DO YOU SPEAK

SPEAK

DIGITAL?

Other Books

Jeremy Schreifels
Road to 99

Aaron Gear
The Future of YouTube | Leveraging AI for Unbeatable Content and Account Management

Other books by Thr33 Kings Media

Coloring Books:
Adult Coloring Book: Reflections of the Year
Childrens Coloring Book: Winter Wildlife

Aaron Gear
Jeremy Schreifels

DO YOU SPEAK DIGITAL?

Publisher Information
Published in the United States of America
Thr33 Kings Media, LLC
602 2nd Ave NE
St. Joseph, MN 56374

Edition Notice
First Printing
November 2023

***Cover Designer* Jeremy Schreifels**
***Book Interior Designer** Thr33 Kings Media, LLC*
***Editor** Thr33 Kings Media, LLC*

ISBN number : 9798867910297
Library of Congress Control Number: 2023922160
***Printed in** United States of America*

www.hustletoelevate.com

Author's Note

The author reserves all rights to be recognized as the owner of this work. No part of this publication may be reproduced, stored in a retrieval system, or transmitted in any form or by any means, electronic, mechanical, photocopying, recording, scanning, or otherwise, without the prior written permission of the author.

This publication is designed to provide accurate and authoritative information in regard to the subject matter covered. It is sold with the understanding that neither the author nor the publisher is engaged in rendering legal, investment, accounting, or other professional services. While the author has used their best efforts in preparing this book, they make no representations or warranties with respect to the accuracy or completeness of the contents of this book and specifically disclaim any implied warranties of merchantability or fitness for a particular purpose. No warranty may be created or extended by sales representatives or written sales materials. The advice, strategies, concepts, thoughts, and text contained herein may not be suitable for your situation. You should consult with a professional when appropriate. The author shall not be liable for any loss of profit or any other commercial damages, including but not limited to special, incidental, consequential, personal, or other damages. Though authors are consultants, each situation of a person or business is different and the totality of all situations can't be accounted for when writing this book. For advice or consulting on your specific matter, please contact Thr33 Kings Media or Hustle to Elevate.

Prologue

In the opening passages of this exploration, we invite you to join us on an extraordinary journey through the rich tapestry of Natural Language Processing (NLP). This discipline, a fusion of linguistics, computer science, and artificial intelligence, represents a transformative force, redefining our interactions with machines and expanding the horizons of human communication.

Our quest begins with a compelling inquiry: Can machines emulate the depth and nuance of human language? In pursuit of this answer, we trace NLP's ascent from theoretical constructs to the pioneering algorithms that now integrate into the fabric of our daily existence. We chart a course through the annals of natural language processing, from its conceptual inception to its present-day embodiment—a narrative testament to the synergistic power of human innovation and technological prowess.

This prologue lays the groundwork for a story that spans historical milestones and envisions future possibilities, where setbacks are mere catalysts for breakthroughs that advance our journey. It's a call to the visionary, the creator, and the thinker to propel this legacy forward, dismantling communication barriers and fostering machines that not only comprehend but connect with us in profound ways.

We will talk about the myriad of applications NLP is used across various sectors, revealing its role as a cornerstone of disruptive innovation—reshaping information access, bridging linguistic gaps, and enhancing global connectivity. Here, we celebrate the strategic and impactful nature of NLP, thriving on the tenacious spirit of those steering its course.

This overview is an invitation to join the dialogue surrounding NLP, a conversation as dynamic as the languages it seeks to decode. We reflect on the responsibility inherent in harnessing such a powerful tool, considering the ethical implications that weave through the fabric of our digital interactions.

This intellectual voyage, will allow you to recognize the importance of inclusivity and diversity, ensuring that our collective progress encompasses the full spectrum of human experience. This journey is one of resilience and agility, where each chapter propels the story of human advancement through the lens of language and technology.

Together, we stand at the threshold of discovery, where each word penned is a stride towards a future illuminated by the language of innovation and inspiration. This is your invitation to the conversational future, to the unfolding saga of Natural Language Processing, where every page turned heralds the next step in a relentless pursuit of knowledge. Welcome to a journey that promises to be as enlightening as it is inspiring— welcome to the story of natural language processing.

Chapter 1

The Genesis of NLP: A Historical Snapshot

In modern commerce and daily living, Natural Language Processing (NLP) stands as a linchpin of transformation. Unveiling NLP's transformative potential through core mechanisms that fuel its prowess, accentuates its pivotal role in business innovation, and sheds light on how it fosters robust human-machine collaboration. Ethical considerations intertwined with NLP's deployment receive due attention, as does the futuristic vista of global and multilingual conversations. Readers are guided towards mastering and capitalizing on NLP's potential, a journey marked by elucidation and empowerment.

Navigating through the core mechanisms of NLP, we encounter algorithms capable of decoding human language with an acumen hitherto reserved for humans. These algorithms, brimming with potential, harness vast datasets to understand, interpret, and respond to human language in a nuanced manner. Their emergence has catalyzed a seismic shift in how businesses interact with consumers, innovate, and stay ahead in competitive markets.

Today, businesses harness NLP to glean actionable insights from consumer feedback, automate customer interactions, and optimize operational efficiencies. This story elucidates how pioneering enterprises have leveraged natural language processing to revolutionize customer experience, drive revenue growth, and foster a culture of continuous innovation. As algorithms become increasingly more sophisticated, we stand on the cusp of an era where human and machine collaboration transcends conventional boundaries, unlocking untold possibilities.

Ethical considerations form a crucial facet of natural language processing. As machines interpret and respond to human language, concerns surrounding privacy, bias, and misinformation surface. This book underscores the imperative for a balanced approach, where the quest for innovation is tempered by ethical responsibility. Scrutiny of NLP's ethical dimensions serves as a precursor to informed deployment, ensuring benefits are reaped without compromising on moral grounds.

Looking ahead, the promise of global and multilingual conversations beckons. NLP, with its ability to bridge linguistic chasms, holds the key to a world where language ceases to be a barrier. Amidst a tapestry of languages, NLP stands as a harbinger of unity, facilitating seamless communication across geographies. The pathways leading towards this promising horizon, offer a glimpse into a future where NLP catalyzes global discourse, fostering understanding and collaboration on a heretofore unseen scale.

This book aims to serve as a conduit for readers, guiding them towards mastering natural language processing's potential. Through a blend of historical insight, real-world examples, and forward-looking perspectives, readers are equipped with the knowledge needed to navigate the burgeoning field of NLP. One garners not only a profound understanding of NLP's core mechanisms, but a vision of its potential to reshape our world. Through discerning engagement with natural language processing, individuals and enterprises alike stand to forge a future marked by innovation, ethical integrity, and global interconnectedness.

The linguistic theories, especially the original work of Noam Chomsky, offered a structured lens through which to view the intricacies of human language. His theory of transformational generative grammar presented a framework, elucidating how sentences could be generated and understood, a cornerstone in the edifice of NLP. It's this structured approach that seeded the idea of codifying language rules for machines to follow, a precursor to the automated language processing.

Parallelly, connectionist models emanated from a desire to mimic the brain's interconnected neuronal architecture. The fundamental premise being, understanding and processing language is, at its core, a function of myriad interconnected nodes working in harmony. These models were instrumental in propelling forward the notion of neural networks, a cornerstone of contemporary NLP. The neural networks, with their ability to learn from data, iteratively improve, and capture nuanced patterns, significantly advanced the field, making machines more adept at understanding and processing language.

Mid-20th century heralded the advent of machine translation and information retrieval, both innovative in propelling the field of NLP into practical realms. Machine translation, with its ambition to bridge linguistic divides automatically, necessitated an extensive understanding and processing of language, thereby catalyzing advancements in NLP. This venture, aimed at transcending language barriers, sowed the seeds for subsequent developments in language processing and understanding.

Information retrieval, on the other hand, necessitated the efficient and accurate extraction of relevant information from a sea of data. This requirement drove advancements in algorithmic processing of text, making machines more adept at understanding, indexing, and retrieving information based on human language queries.

Together, these early influences coalesced, forming a fertile ground on which the edifice of modern NLP was built. Each development, be it linguistic theory, connectionist models, machine translation, or information retrieval, contributed a crucial piece to the puzzle. Their collective impact catalyzed the emergence of natural language processing as we know it, a field poised at the nexus of linguistic understanding and computational prowess, with the potential to significantly augment human-machine interactions in modern commerce and daily living.

The embryonic stages of NLP during the 1950s and 1960s were marked by a fusion of hope, audacity, and ingenuity. The Georgetown experiment, steered by Warren Weaver, stands as a testament to the early belief in machines' potential to emulate human-like language processing. This experiment not only demonstrated the nascent capabilities of computers in language translation but also ignited a spark that would fuel decades of research and innovation in NLP.

During the same epoch, the inception of early natural language processing systems like the General Problem Solver (GPS) and ELIZA took place. These systems, albeit rudimentary, were the first in showcasing the potential of symbolic reasoning in understanding and processing language. They stood as early harbingers of a world where machines could interact with humans in a linguistically coherent manner.

The convergence of Artificial Intelligence (AI) mand cognitive science with NLP was nothing short of serendipitous. Visionaries like Alan Turing and John McCarthy not only envisaged a future where machines emulated human intelligence but took pragmatic steps towards realizing this vision. The Dartmouth conference of 1956 served as a crucible where ideas on AI and natural language processing were exchanged, refined, and amalgamated, setting a robust foundation for future explorations.

Progress in NLP was anything but linear, marked by significant milestones that each added a layer of sophistication to how machines understood and processed language.The Georgetown-IBM experiment stands as a testament to what was achievable, sparking hope and curiosity in equal measure.

As time marched on, statistical approaches and language modeling emerged as powerful tools in the NLP toolkit. The advent of Hidden Markov Models (HMM) was a game changer for speech recognition, ushering in a paradigm where systems could glean meaning from vast swaths of data. This phase also saw machine learning (ML) taking a center stage in NLP, heralding an era where machines could autonomously learn from data, discern patterns, and make informed predictions.

Fast forward to recent years, the renaissance of neural networks and the emergence of deep machine learning have significantly upped the ante. Word embeddings and distributed representations have morphed the way machines perceive and process language, embedding a layer of semantic understanding hitherto unseen. Sequence-to-sequence models have redefined the boundaries of what's achievable in machine translation and language generation, showcasing a glimpse of the immense potential that lies untapped.

In retrospect, the journey of NLP from its humble beginnings to its current state is that of continuous evolution, each phase building upon the previous, driven by a relentless quest for machines that understand and respond to human language with a finesse that rivals, and perhaps someday surpasses, human capability. Through each milestone, NLP inches closer to its ultimate aspiration, forging a future where human-machine interactions are seamless, intuitive, and enriching.

The annals of Natural Language Processing are replete with visionary figures whose ingenuity propelled the field into realms previously unimagined. Each individual, with their unique insights and tireless endeavors, contributed to a legacy that continues to evolve and shape modern human-machine interactions.

Allen Newell and Herbert Simon, regarded as luminaries in cognitive science, were instrumental in grounding the principles of symbolic reasoning and problem-solving. Their pioneering work laid a robust foundation upon which early edifices of NLP and Artificial Intelligence were built. Their pursuit of understanding human cognition and translating these insights into computational models was nothing short of revolutionary.

Marvin Minsky, often hailed as the "father of artificial intelligence," had an indelible impact on both Artificial Intelligence and NLP. His exhaustive work on perception and cognition demystified many complexities surrounding human language understanding, providing a roadmap for translating these intricate processes into machine-readable formats. Minsky's audacious vision of machines mimicking human intelligence was a driving force that spurred numerous advancements in NLP.

Karen Sparck Jones was a titan in the space of information retrieval. Her original work redefined text analysis and indexing techniques, turning them into powerful tools for extracting insights from textual data. The ripple effects of her contributions to statistical language modeling are palpable in modern NLP, where statistical approaches form a crucial backbone in understanding and processing language.

In the contemporary scene, the duo of Yann LeCun and Geoffrey Hinton have emerged as torchbearers of innovation in NLP. Their groundbreaking work on deep machine learning and neural networks has opened new frontiers in the field. The ethos of this learning, underpinned by neural networks capable of mimicking human brain processes, has significantly advanced machines' prowess in understanding and processing human language. Their contributions have not just expanded the horizons of what's achievable but also have enriched the tapestry of methods and models employed in natural language processing.

Together, these key figures constitute a remarkable lineage of thought leadership in NLP. Each, with their unique expertise and vision, carved a path that others followed, setting in motion a cycle of innovation that continues to push the boundaries of NLP. Through their collective endeavors, the dream of seamless human-machine communication inches ever closer to reality, a testament to the remarkable journey NLP has traversed from its inception to its present-day sophistication.

The trajectory of Natural Language Processing reflects a collective endeavor, where institutions and organizations have played pivotal roles in nurturing, advancing, and championing this field. Their contributions have often been the catalysts for innovation, fostering a conducive ecosystem for the exploration and realization of NLP's potential.

IBM Research continues to stand as a hallmark of industrial engagement in NLP. With its long-standing tradition of pushing the frontiers of technology, IBM has made indelible contributions to machine translation and information retrieval. Its endeavors have often translated into practical solutions that underscore the applicability of NLP in solving real-world challenges.

Academic bastions like Stanford University and the University of Edinburgh have emerged as crucibles of innovation in NLP. Their research labs have been fertile grounds where novel ideas are sown, nurtured, and matured. These institutions have been instrumental in cultivating a culture of rigorous inquiry and innovation, propelling the field forward. Moreover, they have been nurturing grounds for talent, producing thought leaders who continue to shape the contours of NLP.

Governmental initiatives have often been the wind beneath the wings of NLP research. Agencies like the Defense Advanced Research Projects Agency (DARPA) have been significant patrons, channeling funds into groundbreaking research. Their backing has often enabled researchers to venture into uncharted territories, unraveling new dimensions of NLP. The infusion of funds, coupled with a vision for technological advancement, has been instrumental in accelerating the pace of research, leading to significant strides in NLP.

In addition, collaborative forums and consortiums have emerged as potent platforms for cross-pollination of ideas across academia, industry, and government. These collaborative ventures often transcend geographical and institutional boundaries, fostering a culture of shared learning and collective advancement.

In totality, the institutional and organizational engagements in NLP have been multifaceted, each contributing a unique strand to the evolving nature NLP has become. They have not only been incubators of innovation but have also played a crucial role in translating theoretical advancements into practical solutions. Their enduring commitment continues to fuel the relentless quest for mastering the intricacies of human language, enabling machines to engage in linguistically rich interactions with humans. Through their collective endeavors, the promise of NLP in enhancing human-machine collaboration and revolutionizing various facets of modern commerce and daily living continues to flourish.

Natural Language Processing has stood, and continues to stand as a quintessential exemplification of interdisciplinary innovation. Its tendrils extend into a myriad of fields, leaving an indelible imprint, facilitating advancements, and reshaping operational paradigms.

In the domain of information retrieval and search engines, NLP acts as a linchpin that has redefined the way we search for and access information. By enhancing the semantic understanding of search queries, NLP has made the retrieval of information more precise and contextually relevant. This transformation is palpable each time we engage with search engines, experiencing a level of responsiveness and accuracy that was hitherto unattainable.

Machine translation and language technologies have been beneficiaries of NLP's prowess. The era of automated translation services, capable of bridging linguistic divides, is a testament to NLP's potential. By automating language translation, natural language processing has not only fostered global communication but also has broken down barriers that once impeded cross-cultural interactions.

Venture into the realms of healthcare, finance, and cybersecurity, and the resonance of NLP's impact is unmistakable. In healthcare, sentiment analysis and chatbots have emerged as conduits for enhancing patient engagement and experience. They provide a semblance of personalization and responsiveness, making healthcare delivery more patient-centric.

Looking at the financial sphere, natural language processing serves as a catalyst for enhancing customer engagement. Chatbots and virtual assistants, powered by NLP, provide instant responses to customer queries, fostering a culture of instantaneity and convenience. Moreover, sentiment analysis helps financial institutions gauge market sentiments, enabling better decision-making.

The cybersecurity domain has witnessed NLP morphing into a sentinel that augments fraud detection and prevention. By analyzing vast swathes of textual data for anomalies and patterns indicative of fraudulent activities, NLP algorithms have become crucial assets in preempting and mitigating cybersecurity threats.

The essence of NLP's influence is of boundless possibilities. Its capabilities have transcended its native domain, seeding innovations in fields far and wide. Each interaction between NLP and these fields has been a harbinger of transformation, opening up new vistas of what's achievable, and setting a trajectory towards enhanced efficiency, accuracy, and user experience. Through these cross-domain engagements, NLP continues to underscore its versatility and transformative potential, embodying a promise of endless possibilities in harnessing the power of language for better human-machine collaboration and decision-making.

We have ventured through time, showcasing the influential ideas and visionary minds that laid the bedrock for this transformative technology. From its embryonic stages marked by curiosity and audacity to its contemporary embodiment replete with robust algorithms and multifaceted applications, the tale of NLP is one of ceaseless evolution.

We looked into the foundational research and the luminaries whose foresight and ingenuity charted the course for NLP's development. Their pioneering work not only unraveled the mysteries of language processing but also set a robust foundation upon which subsequent generations of researchers and practitioners could build.

The milestones we discussed are not mere historical footnotes, but pivotal junctures that shaped NLP's trajectory, each bringing us a step closer to realizing the dream of seamless human-machine communication. The institutions and organizations that took the helm of NLP's developmental voyage were not just catalysts but were crucibles where ideas matured and innovations blossomed.

This chapter took us beyond the confines of NLP, showcasing its far-reaching impact across diverse fields. From revolutionizing information retrieval to fostering global communication and enhancing cybersecurity, NLP's influence is both profound and pervasive.

As we peer into the horizon, the future of natural language processing shimmers with promise. The commercialization of NLP has opened new avenues for business innovation, creating a symbiotic relationship between technological advancement and commercial success. The marriage of NLP with other burgeoning technologies is poised to spawn novel applications that could further redefine the human-machine interface.

As we conclude this chapter, the journey of NLP is far from over. With each passing day, new vistas of exploration open up, beckoning the curious minds to venture forth and unravel the yet-to-be-discovered potentials of NLP. The march of innovation continues unabated, and as we step into the ensuing era, we are reminded that Natural Language Processing is a vivid illustration of human creativity and a glimpse into the extraordinary opportunities awaiting the next wave of innovators. This field stands as a living testament to our ingenuity, continuously unfolding and revealing the vast potential for future advancements.

Chapter 2
Machines that Understand

In chapter 2, we will examine the intricate world of Natural Language Processing —a transformative domain where machines are taught the art of understanding human language. NLP stands as a testament to human innovation, offering a suite of tools and methodologies that allow for intricate interactions between humans and machines across various domains. Here, we shall navigate the essential components of NLP, from syntactic analysis to the marvels of machine translation, unraveling how each contributes to the overarching objectives of artificial intelligence.

As we unfold the layers of NLP, we will discover how it enables machines to parse and interpret the complexities of language, from extracting the sentiment of text to generating language that echoes human thought. The journey will take us through the technical bedrock of NLP, exploring how frameworks like TensorFlow and PyTorch are shaping the future of machine learning and how machine translation systems like Google Translate are dismantling language barriers, promoting a global dialogue.

This chapter aims to illuminate the multi-faceted nature of NLP, providing a lens through which we can appreciate the depth of machine comprehension and the breadth of its applications. As we explore this dynamic field, we will uncover how NLP is not just an academic pursuit but a vibrant, applied science that is revolutionizing how we interact with technology in our daily lives.

Syntax analysis is an essential component of Natural Language Processing, presenting a systematic methodology for dissecting and understanding the structure of sentences. This foundational aspect of NLP is comparable to an intricate journey through a network of linguistic rules and structures, each step designed to uncover a deeper level of complexity inherent in human language.

The process begins with tokenization, a critical initial phase that involves segmenting text into discrete units known as tokens. These tokens, which can be words, phrases, symbols, or other meaningful elements, serve as the fundamental building blocks for subsequent syntactic analysis. By breaking down text into tokens, we establish the groundwork for a more granular examination of the language.

Following tokenization is parsing, a meticulous process where the grammatical structure of sentences is analyzed in detail. This involves applying a set of formal grammar rules to determine how tokens combine to form coherent sentences. Parsing enables NLP algorithms to discern the relationships and dependencies between tokens, effectively identifying the hierarchical architecture that governs the construction of sentences.

An additional layer to this syntactic dissection is part-of-speech (POS) tagging. During this process, each token is meticulously categorized according to its function in the sentence, with labels such as nouns, verbs, adjectives, and more. POS tagging is a pivotal step in the analysis as it provides valuable context regarding the grammatical function and the role each word plays within the sentence's overall structure.

These syntactic analysis capabilities are not merely mechanical processes but represent the initial steps toward endowing machines with a nuanced understanding of language. By mastering these elements of syntax, NLP systems gain a fundamental grasp of linguistic norms, which is an indispensable precursor to advanced levels of text interpretation and processing. This structured approach to language forms the basis upon which more complex linguistic features are explored, paving the way for machines to engage with text in a manner that mirrors human understanding and responsiveness.

Semantic analysis is a transformative step in the journey of Natural Language Processing, where the focus shifts from the rigid structure of sentences to extracting the essence and meaning from the text. But how does this process enable machines to transition from recognizing words and sentences to understanding their context and significance?

Let's consider Named Entity Recognition (NER), which is a pivotal aspect of semantic analysis. Imagine reading an article about the United Nations. Without understanding what "United Nations" signifies, one might just see it as two words placed next to each other. NER, however, identifies "United Nations" as an organization, a key piece of information within the text. This process classifies named entities such as people, organizations, locations, expressions of time, and other significant categories, laying the groundwork for a machine to understand the text's key components.

Moving a step further, Semantic Role Labeling (SRL) takes this understanding to an unprecedented level. If NER tells us 'what' or 'who' is present in a sentence, SRL tells us 'how' these entities are interconnected. For instance, in the sentence "The gardener planted trees," SRL identifies "the gardener" as the doer of the action and "trees" as the recipient of the action. It uncovers the meaning within the text, elucidating the dynamics of actions and the entities involved.

Semantic analysis, therefore, serves as a bridge that connects the dots between structural understanding and meaningful interpretation. This process empowers machines not just to read but to interpret text, allowing them to respond to and engage with human language in a manner that was once the exclusive domain of human cognition. It creates a fluid environment where machines can not only parse the intricate web of human language but also interact with it in a way that is both relevant and contextually informed.

Such capabilities are not just innovative; they are revolutionary. They mark a paradigm shift in how we interact with technology, transforming machines from passive recipients of instructions to active participants in human discourse. Semantic analysis, therefore, is not a mere feature of NLP; it is a foundational component that enables a new era of machine intelligence. It is a testament to human ingenuity and the relentless pursuit of technological breakthroughs that continue to push the boundaries of what is possible.

Sentiment analysis is a pioneering aspect in the field of language processing technology, offering insightful glimpses into the emotional undercurrents within text. It goes beyond merely scanning for explicit expressions, probing into the subtle sentiments and opinions embedded in the language. But what exactly does sentiment analysis entail, and why is it such a game-changer in today's business world?

The technique behind sentiment analysis involves categorizing text. Algorithms in this field, akin to detailed archivists, sift through words to classify them into sentiments—positive, negative, or neutral. This classification is based on identifying linguistic cues and patterns, almost like decoding a language where each word adds to the overall sentiment of the text.

Enhancing this method is polarity detection, where language processing technology moves beyond simple categorization to a more detailed analysis. It measures the intensity of emotions expressed, offering a layered understanding of sentiments. For instance, discerning the difference between a customer stating they are "quite happy" versus "ecstatic" is crucial for businesses analyzing customer satisfaction.

Why is sentiment analysis indispensable? In the current dynamic commercial climate, it serves as a vital tool for understanding consumer feedback. This advanced technology enables businesses to precisely monitor brand reputation and adapt rapidly to feedback. Utilizing sentiment analysis for market insights empowers stakeholders to make informed strategic decisions, creating a culture where customer insights drive innovation and optimization.

Sentiment analysis has transformed how companies interact with customers and analyze the market, becoming a key part of a modern, data-driven business strategy. It illustrates the synergistic relationship between human emotions and machine intelligence, turning each text interaction into a source of actionable insights. Leveraging this technology, businesses not only maintain a competitive edge but also build a legacy of customer-centricity and strategic acumen, excelling in a market where understanding and agility are key to success.

In the intriguing domain of language processing, the generation of language marks a significant shift. Here, algorithms evolve from merely interpreting text to actively creating it, crafting new content with precision and nuance. This capability raises the question: How do machines master the complex task of generating human-like text, and what are the processes enabling this innovation?

A fundamental method used is text concatenation. This involves strategically linking text segments to form sentences and paragraphs that are meaningful and flow naturally, akin to an artisan weaving threads into a cohesive and engaging narrative.

Venturing further into the sophistication of language generation, we find machine learning techniques. These are not just standard algorithms, but advanced systems informed by deep learning that enable a comprehensive understanding of context, semantics, and stylistic elements. In practice, deep learning allows machines to assimilate and replicate the complex patterns of human language, learning from extensive datasets to generate text that resonates with human readers, capturing the essence of human communication.

These methodologies are not just disruptive; they are revolutionary, propelling the field of NLP into new, uncharted territories. Language generation through deep machine learning is a transformative force, enabling machines to produce text that is not only coherent but also rich in variety, adaptable in style, and authentic in tone. From crafting compelling stories to generating precise reports, the applications are as limitless as they are impactful.

Through the lens of language generation, NLP algorithms become more than mere tools; they emerge as digital scribes, pioneering a new paradigm in content creation. This breakthrough has significant implications across industries, revolutionizing how content is created and consumed. As these technologies continue to evolve, they hold the promise of not just mimicking human writing but offering unprecedented assistance in creative and professional domains, driving innovation and empowering users to reach new heights of expressive capability.

As we look further into NLP, we will venture into various branches within this facinating topic. First, we will start with Natural Language Understanding (NLU).

This is a fascinating branch of Natural Language Processing that plays a critical role in how machines interpret our language. The question then arises, how does NLU provide machines with the ability to understand human language? It involves a multifaceted approach to decode the nuances and intentions embedded in text or spoken words.

At the core of NLU is intent recognition. This is where algorithms are trained to discern the user's intention behind their words. Just as a seasoned detective infers motive from actions and statements, NLU algorithms analyze language to understand what users want to achieve. This could be booking a ticket, ordering a meal, or requesting information. Intent recognition is essential because it determines how a system will respond to various requests, ensuring that the interaction is efficient and satisfying for the user.

Alongside identifying intentions, NLU is also adept at entity extraction. Consider this as the process of mining precious details from conversations, like names, dates, and places. These details are the 'entities', and their extraction is akin to pinpointing specific landmarks on a map for future reference. This capability is crucial for systems that need to act on specific user instructions or queries, extracting relevant bits of information from possibly vast amounts of text.

Understanding context is another cornerstone of NLU. Context understanding ensures that the system's responses are not only correct but also appropriate to the current situation or dialogue. This aspect of NLU is like having a keen sense of social etiquette, knowing how to respond not just based on the words spoken but also considering the setting and previous interactions.

Through these mechanisms, NLU empowers conversational agents, such as chatbots and virtual assistants, to engage with users in a manner that's both insightful and relevant. It's the driving force that allows these systems to not just 'hear' but truly understand and participate in conversations. This technology is not just innovative; it's transformative, revolutionizing the way we interact with digital systems. By providing machines with the ability to process human language with such depth, NLU is laying down a benchmark for a future where technology can serve us with a deeper, more intuitive understanding, creating an engaging, proactive, and, ultimately, more human user experience.

Natural Language Generation (NLG) stands as an innovative branch within Natural Language Processing that pushes the boundaries of artificial intelligence. NLG equips machines with the ability to generate text that mirrors human expressiveness and precision. One might ask, how does NLG redefine the interaction between humans and machines? The answer lies in its core functions, which include dialogue systems, content generation algorithms, and personalization techniques.

Dialogue systems represent the forefront of NLG's capabilities, allowing machines to participate in conversations with a level of finesse that was once the exclusive domain of humans. These systems craft responses that are not just coherent but are finely tuned to the context and nuances of the interaction. This capability is transformative, making digital assistants more than mere tools; they become conversational partners capable of understanding and engaging in the ebb and flow of human dialogue.

Content generation is another area where NLG excels. Algorithms within this space can produce a variety of written content, from informative articles to compelling ideas and stories, all while maintaining coherence and engaging the reader. These algorithms are not just prolific; they also embody the tenacity and dedication of a skilled writer, ensuring that every piece of content is not only informative but also resonates with the intended audience.

Personalization is the third pillar of NLG, enhancing the user experience by tailoring communications to individual preferences and contexts. This adaptability makes interactions with machines feel more intimate and relevant, fostering a connection between the user and the technology.

Furthermore, Speech Recognition and Synthesis form an integral part of NLP, facilitating seamless conversions between spoken words and text. Automatic Speech Recognition (ASR) algorithms serve as diligent interpreters, translating the spoken word into written language. Simultaneously, Text-to-Speech (TTS) algorithms are the eloquent orators, turning text into natural and accessible speech. This duality of functions has been pivotal in the development of technologies that we interact with daily, from voice-activated assistants to real-time transcription services.

Lastly, the domain of Machine Translation exemplifies the pioneering spirit of NLP. It encompasses the vision of a world without language barriers, employing various approaches to translate text. Rule-based systems, for instance, are the meticulous scholars, drawing from vast dictionaries and grammatical rules to render one language into another. Statistical approaches, on the other hand, are like the astute pattern recognizers, deducing the best translations from large datasets. Neural Machine Translation represents the zenith of translation technologies, with neural networks that capture and interpret the nuances of language, delivering translations that are not just accurate but are also contextually and semantically rich.

Machine Translation, with its innovative approaches, is a testament to the ingenuity and forward-thinking ethos of NLP, demonstrating its capacity to revolutionize communication and foster a more interconnected global community. In essence, these branches of NLP are not just technological advancements; they are the harbingers of a new era where language is no longer a barrier but a bridge connecting people across the globe.

Automated translation services symbolize the transformative power of Natural Language Processing in creating a world where language differences no longer act as barriers to communication. Machine Translation (MT), as a vital branch of NLP, empowers global interaction and democratizes access to information across cultural divides. But how does MT contribute to global inclusivity and connectivity?

MT, through various NLP tools and frameworks, enables the translation of text from one language to another, thereby facilitating communication between individuals who might otherwise be separated by language. This is not just about replacing words from one language to another; it's about capturing the nuances, idioms, and cultural subtleties of the source language and conveying them accurately in the target language. By doing so, MT has revolutionized the way we consume content, conduct business, and engage with different cultures.

In the arena of text analysis, the process begins with tokenization and part-of-speech (POS) tagging. Why are these steps critical? They lay the foundation for more sophisticated analysis. Tools like the Natural Language Toolkit (NLTK) and Stanford CoreNLP segment text into tokens—words, phrases, or other significant elements. These tokens are the building blocks of language analysis. POS tagging then assigns grammatical labels to each token, establishing the framework upon which further linguistic analysis is constructed. This dual process transforms raw text into a structured form, ripe for deeper examination.

Named Entity Recognition (NER) is another key tool within NLP, focusing on pinpointing and categorizing key information within a text. Why is this significant? Because it allows for the rapid extraction of pertinent information from large volumes of data. Tools such as Spacy and OpenNLP not only identify entities like names and locations but also classify them, providing layers of semantic understanding that are invaluable in various applications such as information retrieval, content organization, and data analysis.

Sentiment analysis, through libraries such as TextBlob and VADER, reveals the underlying emotions and opinions within text. But what is the true value of sentiment analysis? It lies in its ability to gauge public opinion, monitor brand health, and even predict market trends based on the sentiment scores it generates. By classifying text into emotional categories and quantifying sentiment intensity, these tools provide insights that are strategic for businesses and researchers alike, transforming raw data into impactful knowledge.

Language modeling stands as a cornerstone in the field of Natural Language Processing, offering a robust methodology to embed words and phrases with discernible meaning. But how exactly does language modeling contribute to the comprehension of text?

Through techniques such as Word2Vec and GloVe, language modeling advances the capacity of machines to understand and interpret human language. These word embeddings serve a pivotal role by encoding words into vectors, placing them within a multi-dimensional space where semantic relationships can be discerned. This encoding is not arbitrary; it captures and quantifies the nuances of meaning, reflecting how words are used in various contexts. These embeddings are particularly beneficial in enhancing performance in NLP tasks like information retrieval and question answering. But what makes them so effective? They allow machines to grasp subtle linguistic cues that hint at meaning beyond the superficial level, thereby enabling more accurate responses to user queries and facilitating a deeper understanding of text content.

Neural network frameworks, such as TensorFlow and PyTorch, provide the computational architecture necessary for machine learning. Why are these frameworks considered revolutionary? They have democratized the field of machine learning, offering both novices and experts the tools to train, evaluate, and deploy models that are capable of performing a wide array of NLP tasks. Deep learning approaches built on these frameworks have been groundbreaking, enabling advancements in text classification, machine translation, and more by leveraging large datasets and computational power to model complex patterns in language.

When discussing the bridging of language gaps, Machine Translation (MT) systems emerge as transformative tools in global communication. What role do MT systems play in today's interconnected world? Advanced algorithms and comprehensive datasets power systems like Google Translate and OpenNMT, offering unprecedented accuracy in translating text across a multitude of languages. The strategic importance of these systems cannot be overstated—they are game-changers for international business, research, and personal communication, simplifying cross-language interactions and fostering a more interconnected global community.

In essence, each tool and framework within NLP represents a thread in the larger tapestry of language technology. They facilitate the exploration of textual data, enable the extraction of critical insights, and support the construction of applications that leverage language's immense power. Collectively, they form an expansive toolkit, empowering those in the field to unlock new horizons in text understanding and interaction. These advancements not only optimize the efficiency and effectiveness with which we engage with text but also inspire continued innovation in a field that is as impactful as it is prolific.

Concluding Chapter 2, we have journeyed through the expansive field of NLP, uncovering how this technology empowers machines to decipher, interpret, and even generate human language. We have seen the power of word embeddings in providing semantic understanding, the pivotal role of neural network frameworks in machine learning, and the unifying force of machine translation in our globalized society.

Each tool and framework we have explored is a vital component of the NLP toolkit, working in harmony to create systems that can engage with human language in complex and meaningful ways. The insights garnered from these technologies are not merely academic; they are actively shaping industries and enhancing our interaction with the digital world.

As we close this chapter, it is clear that NLP is a field of boundless potential, standing at the crossroads of linguistic mastery and computational innovation. It is a domain that not only optimizes our engagement with technology but also inspires a continual reimagining of the possibilities that lie at the intersection of language and artificial intelligence. With each advancement in NLP, we are reminded of the profound impact that machines that understand can have on society, propelling us toward a future where our digital counterparts are not just tools but collaborative partners in the human experience.

Chapter 3

Navigating Modern Commerce with the Language of Business through NLP

Transitioning from the foundational understanding and core branches of Natural Language Processing elucidated in the previous chapter, we now venture into the pragmatic sphere where NLP intersects with the vibrant domain of modern commerce. The discourse ahead navigates through the conduits of communication that underpin the business arena, unraveling the indispensable role of NLP in enhancing these channels of interaction.

In the dynamic fabric of today's commerce, the essence of business interactions is encapsulated in language. The digital epoch has not only accelerated the pace of commerce but has also elevated the significance of effective communication as the linchpin of business success. Whether it's the dialogue between a business and its clientele, the internal communication among teams, or the insightful information learned from data, language is the common thread that weaves through the tapestry of business operations.

As we look into the various avenues of modern commerce in this chapter, the spotlight will be cast on Natural Language Processing - a technological marvel that stands at the crossroads of language and computation. NLP, with its ability to decipher, interpret, and generate human language, is poised to redefine the contours of business communication. It acts as a catalyst in harnessing the power of language to drive customer engagement, operational efficiency, and data-driven decision-making.

Our goal is to understand how NLP augments communication, and its impact on customer language and the language of data. The narrative ahead will elucidate how NLP transforms mere words into actionable insights, enhances the user experience, and facilitates informed decision-making through data analysis.

The discourse on NLP's relevance in modern commerce is not just a reflection of a technological advancement; it's a voyage into the future of business where the amalgam of human communication and machine understanding fosters a new era of innovation and collaboration. The following sections will unravel the multifaceted role of NLP in modern commerce, shedding light on its potential to propel businesses into a new dimension of operational excellence and customer satisfaction.

Consider the critical role of effective communication in the operations of a business. In the fast-paced exchange of today's corporate world, a competitive edge is secured by those who can articulate their message with both clarity and precision. Natural Language Processing emerges as a transformative tool in this scenario, revolutionizing the way companies automate and refine communication. This innovation not only amplifies the efficiency of discourse within the corporate sphere but also enhances the caliber of engagement with customers and partners. Businesses that implement NLP tools are seen as agile and adaptable, ready to meet the rapid demands of information dissemination and ensuring their messages are accurately interpreted.

A significant challenge for global businesses is the removal of linguistic barriers. With the expansion into diverse markets, companies face a mosaic of languages and cultural nuances that traditional translation methods often cannot efficiently address. Here, pioneering NLP technologies such as Google Translate and OpenNMT provide a breakthrough, effectively breaking down these barriers and enabling seamless communication across linguistic divides. This capability is not merely convenient; it is a revolutionary step towards global inclusivity, allowing businesses to foster meaningful connections regardless of language constraints.

How, then, can businesses harness the insights contained in customer language to drive their marketing and sales strategies? The secret lies in the passion for innovation that NLP embodies. Sentiment analysis, a branch of NLP, unlocks the emotional and opinionated layers within customer language, providing businesses with a profound understanding of customer sentiments. This knowledge is strategic and influential, enabling companies to tailor their marketing efforts, enhance customer experiences, and ultimately, boost their sales. By tapping into the nuances of customer feedback through NLP algorithms, businesses can identify areas for improvement and adapt their offerings to meet customer needs more effectively. This strategic optimization leads to not just temporary satisfaction but the creation of a lasting legacy of customer-centricity and continuous innovation.

The transformative power of Natural Language Processing in the business world extends across various domains, fundamentally altering the way companies interact with data, decipher customer needs, and streamline their operations.

Let's start with the foundational aspect of NLP in business: extracting insights from unstructured data. With the exponential growth of digital communication, data has become more abundant and, paradoxically, more challenging to navigate. This is where text mining comes into play, serving as a bridge between raw data and strategic insight. Imagine sifting through endless digital correspondence to discern patterns or trends. Text mining automates this process, utilizing algorithms to perform entity extraction—which identifies names, places, and organizations within text—topic modeling that reveals prevalent themes, and document summarization to distill lengthy texts into concise summaries.

Natural Language Understanding enhances this process by interpreting the subtleties of human language—its context, connotations, and intent. This is not merely about recognizing words but understanding their significance in varying scenarios. NLU facilitates nuanced interactions, allowing businesses to respond to customer inquiries with a level of understanding that approaches human comprehension. This technology empowers virtual assistants and chatbots to deliver immediate, relevant, and personalized responses, reflecting an understanding of customer needs that was once only possible through direct human interaction.

Diving deeper into sector-specific applications, let's consider e-commerce. Here, NLP serves as a key differentiator in customer experience. Personalization engines powered by NLP analyze customer data to offer tailored recommendations, resonating with individual preferences and past shopping behavior. Furthermore, sentiment analysis tools scrutinize product reviews, extracting not just the content but the emotion behind customer feedback. This informs businesses about how customers feel about their products and what drives satisfaction or dissatisfaction.

In the sector of financial analytics, the impact of language processing technology is equally significant. By analyzing the sentiment in news articles, social media, and expert opinions, algorithms can gauge market sentiment and forecast stock trends, providing investors with a valuable advantage. These tools also scan communication channels for irregularities that might indicate fraudulent activities, thereby serving as protective measures against financial wrongdoing.

Shifting to operations, particularly in supply chain management, this technology simplifies complex procedures by integrating with chatbots and virtual assistants. These handle various tasks, from responding to order queries to managing customer service interactions. Such applications of language processing technology not only save time but also increase accuracy and efficiency, leading to more agile and resilient operations.

In summary, this technology is more than just a tool; it's a transformative factor for businesses. It creates a powerful synergy between technology and language, enabling businesses to innovate, enhance efficiency, and excel in the current competitive environment. Through its innovative methods, companies can extract unprecedented value from their data, forging a more engaging, customer-focused, and intelligent enterprise.

In this chapter, we have explored the language of business and the remarkable relevance of NLP in modern commerce. We have seen how effective communication drives business operations and how NLP-powered machine translation systems break down linguistic barriers in a global marketplace. Furthermore, we have delved into the power of customer language, uncovering the insights gained from analyzing customer sentiments and feedback. Lastly, we have explored how NLP techniques extract valuable insights from unstructured data and transform various facets of business, from e-commerce personalization to financial analytics and supply chain management. By harnessing the power of NLP, businesses can drive innovation, gain a competitive advantage, and thrive in the language-driven universe of modern commerce. In the subsequent chapters, we will further explore the transformative potential of NLP in other business domains, uncovering its applications in customer interaction, fraud detection, information organization, and more.

Chapter 4

Customer Interaction Reimagined

In today's swiftly shifting market, immediate and personalized customer service is not just preferred; it's expected. Chatbots and virtual assistants have emerged as essential tools in this context, reshaping the fabric of customer interaction with remarkable agility. This chapter delves into the transformative synergy between cutting-edge technology and customer service, revealing how chatbots and virtual assistants are not just enhancing but revolutionizing the way businesses engage with their customers.

Through the pioneering lens of Natural Language Processing, this chapter will illustrate how these digital assistants create authentic, responsive, and personalized communication channels. NLP serves as the backbone of this evolution, enabling machines to understand, interpret, and respond to human queries with an unprecedented level of sophistication.

As we unfold the layers of these innovative technologies, we will scrutinize the dual impact of chatbots and virtual assistants: their capacity to streamline customer service operations and their potential to deliver a customer experience that is both engaging and satisfying. This exploration will traverse the practical implications and the strategic deployment of these tools, considering user-centric design and the seamless integration of chatbots into existing customer service frameworks.

Join us on a journey through the intricacies of conversational technology as we dissect the methodology behind the digital revolution in customer service, setting the stage for businesses to embrace these tools and create a legacy of excellence in customer interaction.

To start, lets focus our attention to the dynamic interplay between customers and businesses, which is now redefined by the advent of chatbots and virtual assistants. These innovative tools are reshaping the way we look at and understand customer service, creating fluid environments that cater to the needs of the modern consumer. Chatbots, essentially, are algorithms designed to simulate conversations with users, providing immediate, scripted responses to common inquiries. Virtual assistants, such as Siri and Alexa, are more sophisticated; they not only engage in dialogues but also carry out tasks, drawing on extensive databases and NLP to deliver contextually relevant information.

Why are chatbots and virtual assistants revolutionizing customer service? These technologies empower businesses to meet customer needs with greater agility and precision. Customers today expect swift and accurate assistance; these AI-driven tools deliver just that, around the clock, without succumbing to the limitations of human fatigue. This perpetual availability is transformative, ensuring that a customer in any time zone receives the same level of service as anyone else, at any time.

Moreover, chatbots and virtual assistants offer scalability—a crucial advantage in the face of fluctuating demand. Traditional customer service models require significant investment in human resources, a challenge during periods of high volume or rapid growth. Chatbots and virtual assistants circumvent these constraints, allowing businesses to handle an influx of inquiries without compromising on quality or response time. This is not merely a convenience but a strategic adaptation, reflecting the tenacious and proactive spirit that characterizes today's business leaders.

In what ways do these tools enhance the customer service experience? Beyond providing answers to FAQs, chatbots and virtual assistants guide customers through troubleshooting, offer detailed product information, and assist with order placements. Imagine a customer trying to track an order. Instead of navigating through multiple web pages or waiting on hold, they can simply ask a chatbot and receive an immediate update. This level of service is not only efficient but also empowers customers, fostering a sense of engagement and trust in the business.

Let's consider the practical implications of these technologies. With chatbots and virtual assistants integrated into customer service systems, businesses can deliver personalized shopping experiences, recommend products, and even manage returns and exchanges. These interactions, powered by NLP, are not rigid or impersonal; they're adaptive, learning from each interaction to provide increasingly refined responses. This is where the visionary potential of NLP comes into full view, transforming customer service from a reactive task to a proactive, strategic element of the business model.

In summary, chatbots and virtual assistants are not just incremental improvements in customer service; they are pioneering a new paradigm. By leveraging these tools, businesses can create a distinctive, engaging, and responsive customer service experience. They become more than service providers; they become partners in their customers' journeys, dedicated to creating an experience that is not only satisfactory but truly remarkable. As we continue to witness the expansion and sophistication of these technologies, one can only anticipate the transformative impact they will have on the future of commerce and customer engagement.

To comprehend the intricacies of designing effective conversational experiences with chatbots and virtual assistants, we must begin by addressing a fundamental question: What distinguishes a satisfactory digital interaction from an exceptional one? The answer lies in the meticulous attention to user-centric design—a methodology that places the user's needs and preferences at the forefront of the development process. This approach involves looking at and understanding user feedback, conducting rigorous usability testing, and persistently refining the interface to ensure a seamless and intuitive interaction flow. In essence, the goal is to create an environment where chatbots and virtual assistants not only respond to user inquiries but do so in a manner that feels natural and engaging.

Crafting this intuitive conversational interface demands that these digital conversationalists emulate human-like dialogue, which involves using language that is familiar and easily understandable, avoiding technical jargon that could confuse or alienate users. It's about establishing a rapport with the user, much like a dedicated customer service agent would, ensuring that interactions are not just transactions, but opportunities for positive, meaningful engagement.

Another critical aspect of this design journey is the strategic planning of conversational flows and dialogue. This is where the real 'conversation' begins. The architecture of these interactions often utilizes decision trees or flowcharts, which guide the chatbot's responses to various user inputs. By mapping out these pathways, businesses can create a smooth, logical progression that users can navigate with ease.

However, what happens when a conversation doesn't go as planned? Users might pose questions that fall outside the bot's programmed knowledge or use ambiguous language that the system cannot decipher. This is where robust error handling and fallback strategies come into play. A well-designed chatbot or virtual assistant must be able to handle these unexpected turns gracefully, offering fallback responses or asking clarifying questions that guide the user back on track without frustration.

Personalization is another cornerstone of effective digital interactions. By leveraging user data, chatbots and virtual assistants can offer customized responses, product recommendations, and promotions, much like a seasoned salesperson who remembers a return customer's preferences. This level of personalization isn't just about impressing the user; it's about creating a connection, making each interaction feel as if it's been tailored just for them.

The capacity to retain and utilize context from previous interactions is a testament to the sophistication of modern NLP. When a chatbot or virtual assistant remembers a user's past inquiries or preferences, it eliminates the need for users to repeat themselves, making the conversation more efficient and personable. It's a sign of a system that not only listens but understands and remembers—a trait that defines a truly transformative conversational experience.

In synthesizing these elements—user-centric design, structured dialogue, error management, personalization, and context retention—we create not just a tool, but a conversational partner that can transform the customer experience. It's a journey that goes beyond mere technical implementation; it's about pioneering a new era where businesses communicate with their customers in ways that are engaging, effective, and, ultimately, human. This chapter aims to convey the significance of these elements in creating chatbots and virtual assistants that don't just perform tasks but enrich customer interaction, allowing for a legacy of satisfaction and loyalty.

To further understand how machines can comprehend and mimic human communication, particularly through the lens of chatbots and virtual assistants, a deeper appreciation of the intricate workings of Natural

Language Processing is essential. NLP sits at the heart of this interaction, acting as the engine that powers our digital helpers to respond with a seemingly human touch.

Let's unpack this: Imagine you're interacting with a chatbot about shipping times. How does it understand what you're asking? Through intent recognition, the chatbot interprets your question's purpose—identifying that you're seeking information about delivery. Entity extraction works alongside this, picking out key terms in your inquiry, like 'shipping,' to deliver a relevant response. The chatbot isn't just searching for keywords; it's evaluating the sentence's structure to understand your needs precisely.

But communication isn't just about exchanging information—it's also about understanding emotions. Here, sentiment analysis comes into play. This NLP technique examines the tone of your words, allowing the chatbot to sense your urgency or frustration. By detecting these subtle cues, chatbots and virtual assistants can provide responses that are not just accurate but also empathetic, adapting their tone to fit the context of the conversation.

Now, consider the bot's reply. How does it form a sentence that's natural and engaging? This is where language generation steps in. Trained on vast datasets of human dialogue, Artificial Intelligence models can construct sentences that flow naturally and align with the conversation's context. It's not just about giving you the facts; it's about maintaining a conversation that feels comfortable and human-like.

Tone of voice is another piece of the puzzle. A chatbot for a tech startup might have a casual and friendly tone, while one for a law firm would likely communicate in a more formal and precise manner. This tailored communication style reinforces the brand's image and helps establish a consistent experience across all customer interactions.

When it comes to global reach, multilingual capabilities are key. NLP allows chatbots and virtual assistants to not only translate languages but to understand and respect cultural nuances within communication. These advanced systems can switch between languages seamlessly, making sure that they're not just understood, but that they're also culturally relevant and appropriate.

Through the lens of NLP, chatbots and virtual assistants become more than just automated responders; they are ambassadors of the brand, capable of meaningful and culturally attuned dialogue. They are built to understand the nuance of human language, anticipate needs, and respond in a manner that feels decidedly personal. In essence, NLP doesn't just empower these tools to talk; it enables them to communicate, connect, and create a customer service experience that's both efficient and genuinely human.

To fully comprehend the complexities of how machines, specifically chatbots and virtual assistants, can understand and emulate human communication, one must understand the advanced mechanisms of Natural Language Processing. This exploration begins with a pivotal question: How do chatbots and virtual assistants discern the intent behind a user's message and deliver a coherent and contextually appropriate response?

Addressing this question, it's important to recognize that NLP is the technological foundation enabling chatbots and virtual assistants to process and respond to human language effectively. Consider the scenario of a user asking a chatbot about the status of their delivery. The chatbot employs intent recognition, a cornerstone NLP technique, to interpret the user's request. It's not merely scanning for keywords but analyzing the sentence structure to ascertain the query's intent. Simultaneously, entity extraction pinpoints vital information within the user's message, such as 'delivery status,' facilitating a precise and relevant response.

But what about the tone of the conversation? This is where sentiment analysis becomes instrumental. By evaluating the tone behind the user's text, chatbots and virtual assistants can adapt their responses to better align with the user's emotional state, ensuring an empathetic and personalized interaction. For instance, detecting frustration in a user's message may prompt the chatbot to respond with solutions rather than merely acknowledging the issue.

Next, we consider the bot's reply. How does it formulate a response that seems naturally human? Language generation technologies, powered by Artificial Intelligence models trained on extensive language data, enable the chatbot to construct sentences that are not just grammatically correct but contextually relevant and conversationally fluent. The aim is not solely to provide information but to maintain a dialogue that mirrors human interaction.

The tone of voice used by chatbots and virtual assistants is another facet of NLP at work. It's essential that the digital assistant's language style embodies the brand's character and resonates with its audience. For example, a chatbot for a playful brand may use a more casual tone, while a virtual assistant for a professional service must communicate with formality and precision. By customizing this aspect of communication, businesses create a consistent and brand-aligned experience for the user.

Expanding the reach of these technologies, NLP enables chatbots and virtual assistants to bridge language divides, offering support in multiple languages. Through machine translation and advanced language models, they can converse with users in their native tongue, making interactions more accessible and inclusive. This is not just about translating words but ensuring that the dialogue is culturally aware and relevant.

In essence, through the use of NLP, chatbots and virtual assistants transcend their roles as simple question-and-answer machines. They become sophisticated communicators, capable of nuanced understanding and interaction. Businesses leveraging these technologies can provide customer service experiences that are not only effective and efficient but also deeply engaging and remarkably human. This fosters an environment where customer relationships can thrive, powered by machines that understand the art of human conversation.

To foster an understanding of the optimal deployment of chatbots and virtual assistants, one must examine the best practices that lead to their success in enhancing customer interactions. Let's pose a fundamental question: What strategic approach should businesses take to ensure the effective integration of chatbots within their customer service frameworks?

The answer lies in adopting a progressive, feedback-driven methodology. Initially, businesses are encouraged to start with a modest implementation. This targeted approach allows for the collection of vital user feedback in controlled environments. As an example, deploying a chatbot to handle a specific customer service scenario, like tracking orders, can reveal crucial insights into the user experience. This feedback serves as a guidepost for iterative enhancements, ensuring the chatbot aligns with customer expectations and business objectives. Such incremental innovation is a testament to a business's dedication to creating user-centric solutions, reflecting a pioneering spirit in leveraging technology to serve customers.

Monitoring the chatbot's performance continuously is another best practice that cannot be overlooked. Businesses must be proactive in evaluating key metrics such as response accuracy, user satisfaction, and rate of successful issue resolution. This diligent oversight is instrumental in pinpointing areas where the chatbot may require refinements. By employing robust analytics tools, businesses gain the ability to adapt and optimize their chatbot solutions dynamically, an exercise in continuous improvement and a commitment to mastery in customer service.

Furthermore, the integration of chatbots into the existing customer service and CRM systems must be seamless. This strategic fusion ensures that chatbots contribute to a cohesive and personalized user experience. Imagine a chatbot that can access a user's purchase history and preferences from the CRM to provide tailored product recommendations – this is the level of personalization that exemplifies an authentic and transformative customer interaction.

Equally crucial is the safeguarding of customer data. As businesses empower their chatbots with access to sensitive information, establishing stringent security protocols becomes imperative. Adherence to regulations such as GDPR showcases a business's commitment to data integrity and security, fostering trust and establishing a resilient and trustworthy relationship with customers.

In summary, the deployment of chatbots and virtual assistants must be approached with a vision that embraces adaptability, strategic planning, and a commitment to excellence. By starting small, evaluating performance meticulously, integrating systems intelligently, and upholding data privacy, businesses can revolutionize their customer service operations. This approach not only enhances efficiency but also ensures a customer service experience that is both impactful and sustainable, ultimately fostering customer loyalty and setting a benchmark in the industry.

To comprehend the transformative impact of chatbots and virtual assistants on various sectors, we should consider their application in real-world scenarios. How do these advanced tools reshape the landscape of customer service and engagement across different industries?

With e-commerce, virtual shopping assistants epitomize innovation and convenience. These advanced systems harness customer data, including browsing history and purchase patterns, to offer personalized product suggestions. Imagine a virtual assistant that recalls your preference for organic skincare products and suggests new arrivals in that category; this level of personalization enhances the shopping experience, driving sales and fostering brand loyalty. This is not merely about pushing recommendations but about creating an engaging and seamless journey for the shopper, one that mirrors the expertise of a dedicated salesperson.

Moving to the domain of customer support, Artificial Intelligence-powered helpdesks represent a breakthrough in operational efficiency. By automating responses and guiding customers through self-service options, these helpdesks reduce the need for live agents for common issues. The key here is the intelligent routing of complex issues that require a human touch to the appropriate personnel. This dual approach of automation and human expertise ensures that customer support is both agile and empathetic, striking a balance between efficiency and personalized care.

In the travel industry, conversational travel guides are a game-changer. These chatbots act as personal travel consultants, offering real-time updates on flights, personalized travel suggestions, and assistance with bookings. For a user planning a trip, a chatbot can provide a tailored itinerary based on their interests, such as suggesting a quiet beach getaway or a vibrant city tour, complete with attraction recommendations and dining options. This creates an exclusive and enriched travel experience, making the entire process more enjoyable and less cumbersome.

Each of these case studies underscores the strategic application of chatbot and virtual assistant technology in revolutionizing customer interaction. By crafting experiences that are engaging, personalized, and efficient, businesses not only meet customer needs but also exceed expectations. This exemplifies the power of technology to innovate and empower, transforming how industries operate and how customers interact with brands. With their ability to create fluid, responsive, and proactive interactions, chatbots and virtual assistants are truly pioneering a new paradigm in customer service.

In traversing the dynamic terrain of chatbots and virtual assistants, this chapter has illuminated their influential role in crafting a new era of customer service. These digital intermediaries, underpinned by the robust framework of NLP, offer businesses an unprecedented opportunity to engage with customers in a manner that is both efficient and profoundly personalized.

We've traversed the pathway from the strategic deployment of chatbots to the real-world applications that have set a new benchmark in customer interaction. The case studies presented demonstrate the remarkable adaptability and potential of these tools to empower businesses across various sectors—e-commerce, customer support, and travel—pioneering a service that transcends traditional boundaries.

In conclusion, the integration of chatbots and virtual assistants into the customer service framework is not a mere trend; it is a strategic move towards a future where seamless, responsive, and personalized service is a fundamental business tenet. As businesses continue to innovate and adapt these tools, they are creating a customer service environment that is not just reactive but visionary, setting a new standard for customer engagement and satisfaction. As we look ahead, the evolution of chatbots and virtual assistants promises endless possibilities, where the customer experience is not just enhanced but transformed, propelling us towards a future where excellence in customer service is not the exception but the norm.

Chapter 5

Unveiling Business Intelligence through Insightful Analytics

In this chapter, we will look at the enlightening world of business intelligence and customer feedback analysis. Furthermore, this chapter will help illuminate the path for organizations seeking to navigate the complexities of market trends, customer needs, and informed decision-making. Here, we unravel the intricate tapestry of business intelligence, a critical component in charting a course towards market leadership and innovation.

We will focus on the invaluable treasure of customer feedback, the very lifeblood of business intelligence. It's in the nuances of customer voices and sentiments, captured and analyzed through the lens of Natural Language Processing, where the true power of informed decision-making lies. This exploration unveils how businesses can transform the raw, often untamed data of customer feedback into strategic insights, guiding their journey towards agility, customer-centricity, and innovation.

In this exploration, we will navigate the complex yet fascinating world of sentiment analysis. This sophisticated arm of NLP enables businesses to decode the emotional undertones in customer feedback, offering a deeper understanding of the market's pulse. From the foundations of sentiment analysis techniques to the challenges of language ambiguities and contextual interpretation, this chapter sheds light on the nuances of transforming subjective opinions into objective data.

This journey through the dynamics of customer feedback and sentiment analysis is not just about understanding text; it's about tuning into the customer's voice, empathizing with their experiences, and aligning business strategies with their evolving needs and desires. As we traverse this path, we uncover how sentiment analysis enriches business strategies with a human touch, propelling organizations towards empathetic and data-driven decision-making.

Let us set sail on this insightful voyage, exploring the symbiotic relationship between business intelligence, customer feedback, and sentiment analysis. As we do, we'll discover how these elements intertwine to create a comprehensive strategy that not only resonates with the customer's voice but also drives businesses towards a future marked by innovation, empathy, and strategic foresight.

Business intelligence emerges as a linchpin in strategic decision making. It unlocks a world where insights gleaned from data become the compass guiding organizations towards a competitive vantage point in the market. With business intelligence, the veil over market trends lifts, anticipation of customer needs sharpens, and decision-making transcends intuition to become data-driven. In the swiftly evolving business environment of today, business intelligence propels organizations along the trajectory of success.

Transitioning from the broader scope of business intelligence, the spotlight now falls on a specific, invaluable source of insight - customer feedback.

The voice of the customer, encapsulated in feedback, presents a treasure trove of information waiting to be deciphered. By understanding customer sentiments and opinions, a spectrum of insights into customer preferences, satisfaction levels, and pain points unveils itself. This goldmine of feedback morphs into a lever for driving product enhancements, enriching customer experiences and tailoring marketing endeavors to resonate with the audience. The magic of Natural Language Processing shines through in this venture. Techniques like sentiment analysis and trend identification deployed by NLP enable businesses to distill meaningful insights from customer feedback at an unprecedented scale.

As we pivot from the overarching role of business intelligence to the nuanced analysis of customer feedback, a narrative of informed, agile, and customer-centric decision-making unfolds. It will underscore the transformation of raw data and customer voices into actionable business intelligence, steering organizations towards an informed, competitive, and innovative business paradigm.

Venturing into sentiment analysis, often synonymous with opinion mining, unveils a process dedicated to extracting subjective nuances from textual content, shedding light on the emotions and opinions articulated by individuals or collectives. This endeavor employs Natural Language Processing techniques to autonomously discern whether a text exudes positive, negative, or neutral sentiment. This allows for a clearer picture of businesses gaining a clearer understanding of customer perceptions towards their offerings and overall brand aura.

Transitioning to the technical side of sentiment analysis, a myriad of techniques surfaces, each with its distinct approach. On one hand, supervised learning anchors itself on labeled data, forming a training ground for models to learn from annotated sentiments accompanying text samples. On the flip side, unsupervised learning seeks to uncover patterns and relationships nestled within the data, aiming to identify sentiments. The story progresses, highlighting lexicon-based methods and machine learning algorithms as common protagonists in classifying texts based on sentiment, forming the technical backbone of sentiment analysis.

Yet, as with any analytical endeavor, sentiment analysis too faces its share of hurdles. Language, with its inherent ambiguity and penchant for sarcasm, presents a testing ground for NLP algorithms. The quest for accurate sentiment analysis calls for models adept at interpreting subtle linguistic cues while comprehending the sentiment's context. Context emerges as a key player, often shaping the sentiment expressed, thus necessitating a broader lens through which the text is analyzed. Addressing these challenges morphs into an essential step towards refining sentiment analysis, thereby enriching the gleaned insights.

As we explore the basics, techniques, and challenges of sentiment analysis, a picture of an analytical tool capable of understanding the heart of customer sentiment emerges. It's not merely about analyzing text but about tuning into the customer's voice, understanding their needs, and aligning business strategies to resonate with customer sentiments. Through the lens of sentiment analysis, businesses gain not just data, but insights enriched with human emotion, propelling them towards more empathetic and informed decision-making.

Navigating through the vast expanse of customer feedback, businesses stumble upon a treasure trove of information awaiting exploration. The adventure begins with text mining, a branch of NLP, dedicated to extracting nuggets of valuable information from the labyrinth of unstructured text data. Data preprocessing takes center stage, identifying keywords and topics, and painting a clearer picture of the patterns and insights embedded within the tapestry of customer feedback.

As the journey progresses, the spotlight shifts to specific NLP techniques poised to unveil trends and patterns cradled within customer feedback. Topic modeling steps into the limelight, orchestrating a dance of discovery to unravel latent topics or themes dispersed across a collection of documents. Parallelly, clustering algorithms curate gatherings of similar texts, creating a window for businesses to peer into common issues or emerging trends resonating among customers. The saga continues as these techniques open doors to a deeper understanding, revealing customer preferences, pain points, and the whisper of emerging trends.

Venturing further, the influence of context and external factors in the art of trend identification. The lens widens to encompass external data sources like social media trends and market research, adding layers to the understanding of customer sentiment. The tale spins a web of interconnected factors as market trends and industry developments enter the fray, casting ripples through customer sentiment. Engaging in this broader chronical, organizations find themselves better equipped to draw accurate predictions, adapting their strategies with a finesse tuned to the rhythm of both internal and external influences.

Often businesses find themselves on a quest not merely to listen, but to understand. To sift through the cacophony of feedback, unearthing trends that echo the voices of customers. And as organizations look into the essence of customer sentiment, the curtain rises on informed strategies, aligning businesses with the beats of market trends and customer desires. Through the lens of trend identification, the strategy of business evolves, rooted in a richer understanding of the market's pulse and the whispers of customers.

As we navigate product development and innovation, organizations turn to the compass of customer sentiment and feedback. This venture into the minds of customers unveils their needs, preferences, and pain points, serving as a roadmap to innovation. With this acquired knowledge, the path to crafting products that resonate with customer desires becomes less obscured, fueling the competitive spirit of businesses in the bustling market.

As we continue down this path, the lens shifts to the heart of customer experience and satisfaction. The tool of sentiment analysis, akin to a mirror, reflects the real-time emotions of customers. The reflection reveals the contours of customer sentiment, captured through the lens of social media and customer reviews. This newfound understanding paves the way for tailored customer service strategies and refined marketing messaging. Each adjustment, a step towards crafting personalized experiences, nurturing the seeds of customer satisfaction.

With the tale progressing, the spotlight transitions to the stage of marketing and sales strategies. The script of customer reviews and feedback divulges the strengths and weaknesses of products, echoing the sentiments of the market. A closer look at customer perceptions through sentiment analysis sharpens the focus on marketing campaigns and messaging, revealing room for refinement. The storyline evolves with each gleaned insight, guiding the fine-tuning of marketing strategies and audience targeting. The ripple effect of these adjustments cascades through marketing and sales realms, nurturing better customer engagement and blossoming revenues.

Thus, as the saga of insightful analytics in business unfolds, the narrative escorts organizations through the alleys of innovation, the hallways of customer satisfaction, and the bustling marketplaces of enhanced marketing strategies. The tale illustrates a journey, powered by the essence of understanding, leading businesses towards a horizon of customer-centric operations and data-driven decisions.

Within the warm embrace of the hospitality industry, customer satisfaction reigns supreme. Through the lens of sentiment analysis, hotels and resorts gain a real-time pulse of guest sentiment. This mirror reflects areas yearning for a touch of refinement in service delivery. Addressing guest concerns with a prompt charm, elevating customer experience. A story unfolds where each chapter, guided by insights from sentiment analysis, cherishes guest satisfaction and loyalty, painting a picture of hospitality where every detail is tended to with care.

The technology sector emerges as a protagonist driving the tale of product innovation. The feedback from the cohort of users, a treasure trove of insights, whispers the desires and pinches of the user journey. Through the lens of sentiment analysis, user preferences and pain points unfolds. As organizations draft new chapters of features and enhancements, the plot thickens. The tale now breathes innovation, guided by the compass of customer feedback, as technology companies navigate the competitive waters, offering solutions that echo the desires of their customer base.

The tapestry of case studies continues to enrapture as the spotlight shifts to the bustling stage of e-commerce. Here, the rhythm of customer feedback orchestrates the melody of marketing strategies. The resonance of sentiment analysis unveils product strengths and weaknesses, crafting a vision that guides marketing, messaging and targeting. The e-commerce saga unfolds with each refined strategy, connecting with the hearts of the target audience. As the melody of sentiment analysis plays on, it orchestrates a symphony of enhanced connections and blossoming sales, concluding a chapter where understanding customer sentiment scripts success stories across industries.

Navigating the labyrinth of customer feedback to extract business intelligence warrants a keen eye on the compass of ethics, with privacy and data protection as the cardinal points. The sanctity of customer data demands a meticulous approach from organizations, embracing the ethos of ethical data handling and adherence to the tight-knit fabric of data protection regulations. Business intelligence is woven in elements of data security measures, consent, and anonymization, crafting a tapestry that beholds customer trust and privacy as the prized jewels.

Amidst this, transparency emerges as a leader of responsible insight derivation. It scripts a dialogue of trust between businesses and customers, narrated through the clarity of purpose and methodology of data analysis. The pages of this narrative are turned with articulate communication on data usage, etching the path for responsible insight utilization. The tale hence spun, is one of ethical business intelligence, where transparency isn't merely a character, but the narrator guiding organizations towards a horizon where insights drive harmonious outcomes, both for the business tableau and the chorus of customers.

As we draw this chapter to a close, we reflect on the rich insights and strategic pathways it has unveiled. We have discussed the multifaceted landscape of sentiment analysis and its profound impact on business decision-making. We have seen how, in the hands of skilled practitioners, customer feedback transforms from a cacophony of voices into a symphony of actionable insights, driving product innovation, customer satisfaction, and tailored marketing strategies.

We have seen some of the techniques of sentiment analysis, exploring how it dissects and interprets the emotional undercurrents of customer opinions. The chapter has highlighted not only the potential of sentiment analysis to revolutionize customer understanding but also the challenges it faces - from linguistic nuances to contextual comprehension. Through this exploration, we have gained a comprehensive understanding of how sentiment analysis, as a cornerstone of business intelligence, can act as a guiding star for organizations in their quest for market relevance and customer alignment.

Furthermore, we have ventured across various sectors, witnessing the transformative power of customer feedback in shaping product development, enhancing customer experiences, and refining marketing and sales strategies. From the hospitality industry to e-commerce, the application of sentiment analysis has demonstrated its versatility and critical role in scripting success stories across industries.

In concluding this chapter, we emphasize the importance of ethical consideration in navigating the vast amounts of customer data. We underscored the need for transparency, data security, and ethical data handling as fundamental to maintaining customer trust and upholding the integrity of business intelligence practices.

As we close this chapter, it's clear that the journey through business intelligence and sentiment analysis is not just a path to better data comprehension, but a voyage towards building more empathetic, customer-centric, and innovative organizations. In the world of business, where customer feedback is important to insight, sentiment analysis stands as a powerful tool, guiding companies towards a horizon of informed strategies and resonant customer connections.

Chapter 6

Automating Efficiency: NLP in Operations

As we turn the page from uncovering insightful analytics, our story transitions into a new arena where efficiency takes center stage, orchestrated by the conductor of automation, Natural Language Processing. The journey we embarked upon in the previous chapters leads us to a precipice where we now gaze upon the expansive world of operational optimization. We've navigated the pathways of sentiment analysis, tread upon the stepping stones of trend identification, and witnessed the symphony of success stories where business intelligence played the maestro. The tale spun thus far has been one of harnessing the whispers in data, of tuning into the subtleties of customer feedback to compose melodies of informed decision-making.

Now, as the curtain rises on Chapter 6, we venture into the domain of operational excellence, where the rhythm of routine tasks finds a partner in the dance of automation. The stage is set for NLP to choreograph a ballet of streamlined processes, where each pirouette unveils a layer of efficiency, each leap strides towards data-driven decisions. The spotlight now shines on the act of automating efficiency, with NLP playing the protagonist.We will move through the orchestration of routine tasks, highlighting opportunities to increase efficiency, streamline processes, and draw actionable insights from unstructured data. As we progress, we'll uncover the blueprints of success stories where Natural Language Processing has written narratives of operational excellence. These accounts will resonate with the rhythm of real-world applications, creating a harmonious link between NLP and various aspects of business operations.

Mastering the nuances of operational efficiency is crucial in business today. When talking about workflow efficiancy, Natural Language Processing, plays a pivotal role in allowing these efficiancies. But how does NLP reshape workflow efficiency, and what are its implications for businesses? Let's take a look.

NLP stands as a revolutionary force in the arena of workflow optimization. By automating tasks that involve reading, interpreting, and responding to human language, NLP opens up new horizons of productivity. The transformation lies in its ability to process and understand the complexities of natural language, transforming a simple text stream into actionable insights. This technology not only accelerates processes but also mitigates the risk of human error, ensuring accuracy and consistency in outcomes. By transferring routine, text-driven tasks to sophisticated NLP algorithms, organizations witness a dramatic reduction in errors, thereby enhancing their operational efficiency.

A striking aspect of NLP's contribution is in liberating human intellect from the confines of mundane tasks. With routine processes automated, professionals can redirect their focus towards areas requiring strategic thinking, innovation, and creativity. This shift represents not just an operational change but a paradigm shift in how work is approached and executed. NLP, in this regard, acts as a steward of mundane tasks, performing them with unparalleled precision and speed, previously unattainable in manual processing.

Furthermore, NLP transforms the dynamics of workflow, transitioning from the cumbersome processes of manual text handling to a more agile and efficient automated system. This change isn't just about faster processing; it's about redefining the rhythm of work to resonate with enhanced productivity and diminished error rates. NLP offers a new perspective on achieving operational excellence, setting the stage for continuous improvement and optimization.

As we progress in this chapter our focus shifts to exploring real-world applications of NLP. Each example will underscore the symbiotic relationship between NLP and enhanced operational efficiency. Our journey through these applications is not just about comprehending a technology; it's about recognizing and harnessing its potential for bringing about transformative changes in business operations. NLP is emerging as more than just a tool—it's becoming a pivotal element in shaping a business world where efficiency and productivity are not mere aspirations but tangible realities.

In today's data-driven era, the ability to interpret unstructured data stands as a significant challenge for businesses. Amidst the vast expanse of text data lies a treasure trove of insights, yet to be uncovered. Here, NLP serves as a vital instrument, a guiding light in the exploration of this extensive unstructured text. It empowers businesses to wade through complex data, aiding in the enhancement of decision-making processes. By translating the intricate language of unstructured data into actionable insights, NLP is playing a critical role in enabling businesses to not only understand but effectively utilize the wealth of information at their disposal. This capability of NLP to decode and make sense of extensive text data is not just about processing information; it's about transforming how businesses operate and make decisions in an increasingly information-saturated world.

The quest to extract meaning from text begins with sentiment analysis. This technique is not just about recognizing words, but about discerning the emotions they convey. For instance, when analyzing customer feedback or social media discussions, sentiment analysis provides a clear picture of customer feelings and opinions. This critical insight is invaluable for businesses to align their products and services with customer emotions and preferences.

Further along this journey, text classification serves as a key ally. It methodically categorizes text into specific groups, offering a structured view of what might otherwise be a chaotic array of information. This approach is especially effective in organizing diverse data types like customer inquiries, emails, or product reviews. By deploying text classification, businesses employ NLP to bring order and clarity, one category at a time.

Textual data allows entities such as names, places, and organizations play crucial roles. Entity recognition is the tool that identifies these elements, providing vital context within the text. Understanding the specific subjects of a text enhances comprehension, enabling diverse applications from enhancing customer service to informing market research strategies.

The endeavor of mining meaning from unstructured data resembles a quest for hidden treasures. As businesses traverse the labyrinth of text data, NLP acts as a guiding compass. Each sentiment analyzed, every text classified, and each entity identified marks a step closer to uncovering patterns and insights previously obscured. These discoveries become beacons, guiding businesses towards more informed and strategic decisions.

This journey with NLP transcends mere text interpretation; it's about uncovering the hidden data within. The real prowess of NLP lies in its ability to turn pages of text into a wealth of insights, each word serving as a marker leading to a deeper understanding of customer behaviors, market trends, and operational efficiencies. NLP transforms unstructured data from an overwhelming challenge into a valuable asset for businesses, fostering a culture where informed decisions are the norm. This shift towards leveraging comprehensive data insights positions businesses for heightened success when it comes to competitive, information-rich operations.

In any business, demand forecasting is an important concept to understand and use. This concept is akin to a script that orchestrates the delicate balance between supply and demand. Its fundamental goal is to anticipate future requirements for products or services, which is essential for optimizing operations, managing inventory effectively, and maintaining customer satisfaction. However, this script is often complicated by the fluidity of human behavior and market variables. It's in this complex scenario that NLP makes its entrance. With its capability to process and analyze textual data, NLP provides insights into customer sentiments and evolving market trends. By interpreting customer feedback, news articles, and market reports, NLP aids in constructing a more accurate and dynamic picture of future demand, enabling businesses to make strategic decisions based on a comprehensive understanding of market forces.

One wounder, how does NLP enhance the art of demand forecasting? The answer is found in its capacity to analyze the extensive array of customer reviews, social media conversations, and feedback. This thorough examination of extensive data sources enables more precise predictions and informed strategy formulation in business operations by using these algorithms to uncover underlying customer preferences and potential shifts in demand. This insight is invaluable, acting like a ripple in the market's pond, influencing and refining demand forecasting models to increase their accuracy and relevance.

Furthermore, NLP champions the often-overlooked feedback loop. Through detailed analysis of customer feedback, it uncovers hidden insights about market needs and product perceptions. Integrating this feedback into demand forecasting models sharpens their predictions, aligning them more closely with real market conditions.

As traditional methods of demand forecasting make way for natural language processing powered techniques, we witness a significant transformation. The agility and precision introduced by these techniques are not just technical upgrades but strategic enhancements. This accurate demand forecasting resonates throughout inventory management systems, mitigating the risks of excess stock or shortages and thus painting a picture of enhanced profitability and efficiency.

Natural language processing in demand forecasting is one of a transformative era, where traditional methods are replaced by a new dawn of insight-driven forecasting. Through NLP, the future of demand, once clouded in uncertainty, becomes illuminated with data-driven insights. This advancement is a technological leap and strategic cornerstone, essential for businesses to thrive in competitive markets. In this new era, NLP stands as a luminary, guiding businesses with precision and insight, shaping a future where data-driven decisions lead to operational excellence and market success.

Transitioning from demand forcast, to In the intricate area of supply chain management, a vital component in the symphony of business operations, natural language processing emerges as a transformative force. It's poised to redefine the dynamics of supply chain visibility and real-time tracking, crucial in the seamless flow of procurement, production, and delivery. This innovation represents a paradigm shift, where traditional processes meet the pioneering spirit of NLP, revolutionizing how businesses handle the complex dance of their supply chain.

How does NLP create a revolution in supply chain management? It starts with the automation of procurement processes. NLP transforms the interpretation and processing of procurement documents, creating a fluid and agile environment. Requisitions, purchase orders, and supplier communications are no longer mired in complexity but glide through with unparalleled efficiency. This automation is a strategic game-changer, significantly reducing costs and paving the way for streamlined operations and financial prudence.

As we look closer into the supply chain vertical, NLP's role in inventory optimization comes to the fore. By decoding unstructured data, NLP empowers businesses to gather insights from a diverse array of data sources. This capability enables a strategic, data-driven approach to inventory management, effectively minimizing costs and maximizing operational efficiency.

Supply chain management isn't complete without acknowledging NLP' ability to identify potential disruptions. By sifting through vast quantities of data, sheds light on hidden risks and enables businesses to be proactive in averting operational disruptions. This forward-thinking approach is essential in today's fast-paced business environment, where adaptability and resilience are key to success.

In a world where real-time tracking is essential, NLP is the trailblazer. It revolutionizes the monitoring and analysis of supply chain data, laying the groundwork for unprecedented visibility. NLP sets a new benchmark in operational excellence, transforming supply chain management into a more agile, resilient, and efficient process.

Turning to customer service, sentiment analysis, another facet of NLP, stands as a crucial tool in optimizing customer interactions. Exceptional customer service is a hallmark of distinguished businesses, where understanding the customer's voice is critical. Sentiment analysis delves into customer feedback, extracting emotional insights from reviews, surveys, and social media interactions. Through NLP, customer sentiments transcend words, offering tangible metrics for businesses to act upon.

This process is not just about analysis; it's about transforming insights into personalized customer interactions. It's a resonant echo of understanding and appreciation, reflecting a business's dedication to customer satisfaction. Furthermore, sentiment analysis acts as a strategic compass, guiding businesses towards areas needing improvement. This feedback loop is vital for businesses to evolve, aligning their services with customer expectations and fostering a sustainable, prosperous customer service environment.

In the dynamic sphere of customer support, the introduction of NLP-powered chatbots represents a transformative wave, revolutionizing the way businesses interact with their customers. These digital pioneers, adept at understanding customer intent, have redefined customer interactions, offering swift, accurate, and engaging responses. This development raises a pertinent question: how do chatbots powered by NLP enhance customer support experiences?

The answer lies in the unparalleled efficiency of these chatbots. By interpreting customer queries in real-time, they provide immediate responses, crucial in an era where promptness is synonymous with satisfaction. This aspect of NLP-powered chatbots is a strategic breakthrough in minimizing response times, a key factor in fostering customer satisfaction and loyalty. Their ability to not only understand but also provide relevant solutions to customer queries underscores the innovative strides being made in customer support. By grasping the essence of customer concerns, NLP chatbots deliver solutions that precisely meet customer needs, thereby cultivating an environment of excellence in customer support. In essence, the synergy between NLP and chatbots is a game-changing force in customer support, heralding a new era of streamlined, efficient, and customer-centric support systems.

Natural language processing emerges as a luminary in guiding businesses through the complex maze of regulatory frameworks of Quality Assurance (QA) and compliance. In this intricate domain, the role of NLP is pivotal. It casts light on potential anomalies and deviations in processes or products, facilitating compliance and quality assurance with its textual data analysis expertise. For instance, NLP's ability to dissect vast amounts of textual data generated during various stages of product development and operational workflows is a bold step towards risk reduction. Imagine NLP scanning thousands of product reviews to identify potential quality issues – this capability not only saves time but also has a significant impact on maintaining high-quality standards.

Regulatory compliance is another area we can see natural language prossesing being used. By analyzing documents, reports, and communications against established compliance benchmarks, NLP can proactively identify potential red flags. This proactive approach revolutionizes compliance monitoring, reducing the risk of non-compliance and its financial implications. Employing NLP in the fast-evolving domains of QA and compliance exemplifies the technological evolution in risk management and regulatory adherence. Through its continuous monitoring and real-time alerts, NLP empowers businesses to remain vigilant and compliant, fostering a culture of excellence and accountability. This strategic implementation of NLP in quality assurance and compliance not only ensures adherence to standards but also positions businesses as leaders in operational excellence and regulatory foresight.

Regulatory compliance requires document management, which natural language processing continues to use, fundamentally altering efficiency and precision. This technology revolutionizes the often tedious task of document classification and categorization, bringing a wave of innovation. By automating these processes, NLP fosters a fluid environment where documents circulate seamlessly, becoming easily accessible and well-organized. This leads us to ponder: How does NLP transform the daunting task of managing documents?

The answer lies in NLP's groundbreaking improvement of search capabilities. With NLP, the once laborious task of finding specific documents becomes a streamlined and efficient process. NLP's understanding of context and semantics reinvents document search, ensuring relevant and precise results, thereby reducing both time and effort in document retrieval. Additionally, NLP exhibits mastery in automating document categorization. It analyzes content, categorizing documents accurately, and making them effortlessly retrievable. This automation significantly reduces administrative load, marking a stride towards heightened operational efficiency. NLP emerges as the cornerstone of modern document management systems, alleviating the inconvenience associated with traditional manual document handling. Its role in automating and streamlining document management serves as an inspiration for businesses striving for operational excellence.

In the sphere of business operations, the automation of tasks and workflows stands as a pivotal element, orchestrating a symphony of efficiency and precision. Here, NLP reveals its strength, enabling businesses to automate repetitive tasks and streamline workflows. The goal extends beyond mere automation; it's about creating intelligent, adaptive workflows that evolve in sync with user preferences, driving businesses towards peak efficiency while showcasing the vast potential of NLP. This silent workhorse of modern enterprises provides relief to human resources, liberating them from monotonous tasks to focus on higher-value activities. Within this framework, NLP acts as a maestro, its algorithms skillfully sifting the expanse of unstructured data, transforming disarray into a well-orchestrated workflow.

Each task automated and each workflow streamlined becomes a testament to efficiency. NLP, with its proficiency in interpreting human language, infuses intelligence into these processes. Unlike the rigid automation systems of the past, current NLP-powered automation demonstrates an understanding and adaptability that aligns with user preferences, fostering an environment ripe for exponential productivity. The methodology employed is both meticulous and agile, pinpointing routine tasks, comprehending linguistic nuances, and automating them with a precision that reflects an extensive understanding of operational needs. It's not about indiscriminate automation, but a discerning approach that identifies, understands, and then automates, ensuring the core of the task remains intact while the execution becomes significantly more efficient.

Furthermore, the impact of such automation extends beyond immediate operational efficiency, influencing customer experience, employee satisfaction, and ultimately, the bottom line. The use of NLP in task and workflow automation is one of crafting a story of operational excellence that aligns with the strategic vision of the enterprise. In the broad canvas of operational management, NLP-powered automation adds bold strokes of efficiency, innovation, and strategic alignment. The transition from task inception to execution becomes less burdensome, more insightful, and highly efficient, thanks to the synergy of NLP and automation. As businesses progress on this journey, the aspiration of reaching the operational zenith transforms from a distant dream into a tangible, attainable reality.

The future of NLP within operations is characterized by the seamless integration of NLP with other groundbreaking technologies, leading to an innovative paradigm where operational processes are not merely efficient but are continuously adapting and evolving.

One might wonder, how will these audacious advancements in NLP shape the future of operations? The answer lies in envisioning a future where operational challenges are transformed into opportunities for achieving unparalleled efficiency. Natural language processing within the sphere of operations is rapidly progressing, each new development bringing with it a promise of further innovation, enhanced efficiency, and an unyielding progression toward a future where operations are not only smart and agile but also proactive in their approach.

In this projected future, staying current with developments in language processing technology is essential for businesses. It's more than just being informed; it's about progressing alongside the wave of innovation. In doing so, businesses place themselves in a position to effectively leverage the transformative capabilities of this technology, propelling their success in a digital environment that is both challenging and filled with opportunities. The envisioned state of operations, as influenced by this technology, represents not just technological progress but strategic foresight, where operations are constantly aligned with the rhythm of innovation, ensuring businesses stay resilient, agile, and leading in an ever-evolving market.

Natural Language Processing continues to redefine operational efficiency in business. From automating routine tasks to deriving deep insights from unstructured data, it stands at the forefront of a new revolution in business operations. Its capacity to understand, interpret, and interact with human language has unlocked new avenues for boosting productivity, influencing strategic decisions, and fostering more dynamic, responsive, and efficient workflows.

Looking towards the future, the potential of this technology in transforming business operations keeps growing. Its integration with other cutting-edge technologies heralds even more innovative and adaptable operational strategies. This evolution is not merely about enhancing current processes but reimagining business operations in a world driven by data and centered on customers. The ongoing progress in this technology will surely introduce new applications, solidifying its role as an essential component in the corporate arena.

For businesses, engaging with Natural Language Processing is a continuous journey that demands commitment to innovation, flexibility, and a forward-thinking approach. Keeping pace with the latest advancements in this field and embracing its capabilities is crucial for unlocking new paths to operational superiority and retaining an edge in the swiftly changing business environment. In its essence, this technology is a catalyst for transformation, a driving force for growth, and a builder of businesses that are prepared for the future. As organizations fully utilize the potential of this technology, they set the stage for a future where operational effectiveness, strategic insights, and customer engagement merge, leading to unmatched business success.

Chapter 7

NLP Protecting Assets in Fraud Detection

As fraud continues to evolve in today's digital age, businesses are facing increasing challenges in safeguarding their assets. The emergence of advanced technologies, such as Natural Language Processing, has provided a powerful solution to detect and prevent fraudulent activities. In this chapter, we will talk about the applications and benefits of NLP in fraud detection, exploring the various capabilities of NLP and how it can help businesses stay one step ahead of fraudsters.

In today's vast network of interconnected domains, the threat of fraud is ever-present, evolving beyond traditional forms of deception into a more complex adversary. With the rise of the digital age, new types of fraud have emerged, including identity theft, phishing scams, and online payment fraud. These deceptions affect not only the financial standing of businesses but also their reputation in the market. Understanding the changing nature of fraud is crucial for companies to appreciate the importance of cutting-edge technologies like Natural Language Processing in combating fraud.

Fraudulent activities have become more sophisticated, with perpetrators using various tactics to penetrate the defenses of businesses. The impacts of these fraudulent acts extend beyond monetary losses, potentially damaging a company's reputation for years. The scope of fraud has expanded from simple deceit to a significant challenge, utilizing digital tools with malicious intent.

This evolution of fraud necessitates a shift in detection and prevention strategies. The situation highlights the need for advanced technological solutions in business defense strategies. Natural Language Processing stands out as a key player in this field, signaling a new era in the fight against fraud.

The capabilities of Natural Language Processing in fraud detection are impressive. By analyzing transactions, communication layers, and user behavior, it acts as a guardian, identifying patterns and anomalies indicative of fraud. The efficiency of algorithms powered by this technology in automating analysis represents a significant advancement, reducing reliance on manual efforts and enhancing accuracy.

With its ability to interpret and understand human language, this technology equips businesses with an alert system, skilled at spotting the hidden threats of fraudsters. The automation it brings to the table is transformative, creating a more secure environment where fraudulent activities are less likely to go unnoticed.

The methodology employed by NLP in fraud detection is a blend of innovation and precision. It delves into the intricacies of language used in transactions and communications, unmasking the veiled indications of deceit. The automation in fraud analysis is not merely about reducing manual efforts; it's about creating a resilient shield, ever vigilant and adaptive to the evolving tactics of fraudsters.

Furthermore, the synergy between NLP and other technological advancements augments the fraud detection capabilities of businesses. It's a bold stride in a domain where the cost of failure is colossal. The adeptness of NLP in identifying potential fraud fosters a proactive milieu, enabling businesses to thwart fraudulent endeavors before they inflict damage.

Fraud detection is one of empowerment, innovation, and an unwavering resolve to protect the sanctity of businesses in a digital age where fraudsters are relentless. The ability to adapt, innovate, and remain tenacious in the face of evolving fraud techniques is a testament to the transformative impact NLP has in this domain.

In the quest for optimal fraud detection, sentiment analysis emerges as a crucial knight on the chessboard. Employing Natural Language Processing, enterprises can dissect customer interactions, pinpointing unusual or suspicious sentiments that might be the harbingers of fraudulent behavior. The application of sentiment analysis spans multiple channels, embodying customer support chats, social media utterances, and the myriad of email exchanges. When melded into fraud detection frameworks, sentiment analysis acts as a catalyst, amplifying the precision in flagging fraudulent endeavors.

Unveiling the veil of potential fraud often begins with a discernment of the undertones in textual interactions. Sentiment analysis, with its ability to sift through the tonality, nuances, and underlying sentiments in text, becomes an indispensable tool in the fraud detection arsenal. The methodology deployed extends beyond mere word analysis, looking into the essence of expressions, thereby offering a deeper comprehension of potential fraudulent sentiment.

This technique is not just about identifying negative sentiments but spotting anomalies in sentiment patterns that could signify deceit. The agility of NLP in adapting to diverse textual datasets empowers businesses to create a robust and proactive fraud detection mechanism. In a world where timely identification of fraud can avert substantial financial and reputational damage, sentiment analysis is indeed a game-changer.

Moreover, the synergy between sentiment analysis and other NLP techniques cultivates a more holistic approach towards fraud detection. The trailblazing capability of sentiment analysis to flag potential fraud early in the cycle is a testament to its pivotal role in contemporary fraud detection strategies.

The dominion of unstructured data is a goldmine of insights waiting to be unearthed, particularly in the context of fraud detection. With Natural Language Processing at the helm, businesses can venture into this unchartered territory, extracting pearls of insights from a sea of text, emails, and social media posts. These unstructured data nodes, when decoded, reveal patterns and connections that might indicate fraudulent schemes.

NLP, with its ability to interpret and analyze text, becomes the torchbearer in this expedition, illuminating the hidden corridors of unstructured data. The actionable insights garnered through this process are not mere indicators of potential fraud but a treasure trove of information that can be harnessed to bolster the fraud prevention architecture.

Unstructured data, often deemed as a haystack, hides needles of fraud indicators that NLP techniques can adeptly locate. The process of extracting meaningful insights from such data is a blend of art and science, embodying a methodology that's both robust and agile.

Moreover, the analysis of unstructured data paves the way for a more profound understanding of fraudulent behaviors, facilitating the development of preventative measures that are both effective and adaptive. The ripple effect of insights derived from unstructured data transcends the ladders of fraud detection, fostering an environment where businesses are not merely reactive but perpetually vigilant.

With the progressive march of fraudulent tactics, having a resilient, insightful, and proactive mechanism to analyze unstructured data is no longer a luxury but a necessity. And it's in this arena that NLP shines, promising a paradigm of fraud detection that's as tenacious and innovative as the adversaries it seeks to thwart.

In the financial sector, the vigilance against fraudulent activities is a relentless pursuit. The emergence of NLP (Natural Language Processing) algorithms has been a breakthrough, creating a robust mechanism to detect anomalies in financial transactions. Through meticulous scrutiny of transaction data and its comparison against historical patterns, NLP identifies deviations that often are the footprints of fraudulent activities. The real-time monitoring capability of NLP accompanied by proactive alerts crafts a vigilant environment, enabling businesses to stride ahead of fraud risks.

Natural Language Processing algorithms are not just tools, but vigilant sentinels, meticulously scanning transactions for irregularities. Each detected anomaly is a potential warning, prompting businesses to assess and respond swiftly. The real-time monitoring capability is transformative, fostering a culture of proactive rather than reactive measures. The prompt notifications from these algorithms are crucial, enabling businesses to respond to threats with speed and agility.

Moreover, these algorithms are a source of measurable insights into the likelihood of fraudulent activities. They enable businesses to not only identify but also evaluate and quantify fraud risks. The insights offered by Natural Language Processing are key in developing preventive strategies, effectively shielding business assets.

Risk assessment is the cornerstone of fraud detection, filtering potential threats from countless transactions. With Natural Language Processing at the forefront, businesses can efficiently analyze vast data volumes, identifying high-risk profiles and transactions. The automation of risk assessment by this technology marks a leap towards greater efficiency, reducing manual labor and facilitating informed decisions in fraud prevention.

The efficiency of Natural Language Processing in data analysis transforms risk assessment into a more streamlined process. It goes beyond merely identifying risks to automating their assessment in an efficient and insightful manner. The rapid identification and mitigation of potential risks are defining features of this technology's role in fraud prevention.

With Natural Language Processing, risk assessment becomes empowering, allowing businesses to proactively mitigate risks. The automated risk assessment it provides is not just a method but a strategic approach that strengthens businesses against fraudulent activities. This automation ensures that businesses are not just conducting operations but are orchestrating a secure transactional environment amidst the ever-present risk of fraud.

In the current era of global business expansion, crossing language barriers is common, bringing the challenge of detecting fraud across different languages. Language differences can obscure fraudulent activities, obstructing clear insights into potential deceptions in varied linguistic contexts. Natural Language Processing stands out as an invaluable tool in this area, providing businesses the ability to decipher and detect fraudulent nuances across languages.

NLP is like a linguistic maestro, orchestrating a symphony of languages, deciphering the essence of communication beyond the language barriers. Its prowess in analyzing and understanding multiple languages is transformative, ensuring a comprehensive fraud detection framework irrespective of the linguistic medium employed in fraudulent communications. With NLP, language is no longer a barrier, but a conduit to a more robust fraud detection mechanism.

Multilingual fraud detection empowered by NLP is a strategic asset for businesses eyeing global horizons. It not only amplifies the fraud detection capabilities but significantly contributes to a business's global stance, shielding it from fraud's nefarious grasp. In a world where fraudsters are constantly innovating, the multilingual fraud detection prowess of NLP is an authentic, resilient, and tenacious defense line, ensuring businesses remain prosperous and unscathed amidst linguistic diversities.

The realm of fraud detection amplifies in efficacy when humans and machines join forces. The synergy between human intuition and machine intelligence, particularly NLP, creates a formidable alliance against fraudulent activities. NLP stands as a powerful assistant to fraud analysts, providing a spectrum of tools that streamline the review and validation of potential fraud cases.

In the collaborative theater of fraud detection, NLP-powered tools are the catalysts, accelerating the process of sifting through voluminous data, illuminating patterns, and validating suspicious activities. The dialogue between humans and NLP tools is engaging, each learning from the other, refining the process of fraud detection into a fine art of accuracy and efficiency.

This collaborative ethos redefines fraud detection, propelling it into enhanced efficiency, accuracy, and superior outcomes. The human-machine interaction augments the fraud detection capabilities, ensuring a meticulous, yet swift identification and validation of potential fraud, a strategic approach that leaves no stone unturned.

The quest for fraud detection through NLP, while impactful, necessitates a thorough examination of ethical considerations. Privacy and data protection are the linchpins in deploying NLP for fraud detection. It's imperative for businesses to tread the fine line between vigilant fraud detection and adherence to privacy norms.

Ethical stewardship in NLP fraud detection encapsulates robust security measures, data anonymization, and obtaining the requisite consent from individuals whose data is being analyzed. This balanced approach ensures the individual's rights and legal boundaries are respected, fostering trust and adherence to ethical standards.

In the broader spectrum, ethical considerations in NLP fraud detection are not merely compliance checkboxes but a commitment to uphold the trust and privacy of individuals. It's ability to show accountability and respect towards individual privacy while harnessing the power of NLP to create a secure and prosperous business environment. This balance between security and privacy is the hallmark of an ethical, responsible, and sustainable approach to NLP fraud detection.

As the sinister veil of fraud continuously morphs, finding new conduits to infiltrate, the battle against it intensifies. In this relentless fight, Natural Language Processing stands as a resilient warrior, poised to adapt and innovate. The future heralds a time where NLP doesn't just partake in the battle against fraud; it leads the charge. With fraudsters innovating at a rapid pace, the emergence of deepfakes and AI-generated content presents a new frontier of deceit, one that traditional fraud detection mechanisms find challenging to counter. The anatomy of fraud is complex, but at its core lies communication, often veiled in layers of deceit. NLP, with its ability to decode the essence of language, emerges as a pioneering force in unveiling these layers, offering a glimpse into the true nature of communications. The potential of NLP isn't static; it's a rapidly evolving field, mirroring the fast-growing threat of fraud. As deepfakes and AI-generated content blur the lines between reality and falsehood, NLP's role transcends from being instrumental to indispensable.

Deepfakes, once a term relegated to the annals of science fiction, is today's reality, and a grave one at that. The ability to create hyper-realistic fake videos or audio recordings can be a potent tool in a fraudster's arsenal. Similarly, AI-generated content can impersonate legitimate communication, creating a contained environment for fraud to thrive. These evolving deceit technologies demand an equally agile and innovative response. NLP, with its continuous advancements, holds the promise of being that formidable response. With a legacy of transforming unstructured data into actionable insights, NLP is the vanguard against new forms of fraud. Its ability to scrutinize and interpret natural language is unparalleled, making it an elite choice for discerning the authenticity of digital content. Whether it's distinguishing a deepfake from a real video or identifying AI-generated text, NLP has the potential to be a game-changer.

For businesses, the future involves not just coping with the complexities of fraud detection but excelling in it. The adoption of robust Natural Language Processing technologies has become essential. To protect against emerging fraud techniques, businesses need to be proactive and fully embrace these technologies. This means not only utilizing current capabilities but also fostering a culture of ongoing learning and adaptation to stay abreast of advancements in this field. Combining this technology with solid preventive measures creates a formidable defense against fraud. A comprehensive strategy is essential, which involves educating industry stakeholders, establishing efficient channels for reporting fraud, and promoting a culture of accountability. The approach to combating fraud is clear - a combination of advanced this technology and strong preventive measures, supported by a culture of vigilance and continual improvement. This cohesive strategy is designed to not only anticipate potential fraud but also to build a strong defense, preserving the integrity and trust that are crucial in the digital era.

In conclusion, Natural Language Processing has emerged as a critical ally in the relentless fight against the ever-evolving and increasingly sophisticated world of fraud. Its capabilities in understanding and analyzing the complexities of human language have opened new vistas in detecting and preventing fraudulent activities. From sentiment analysis to unstructured data interpretation, NLP equips businesses with the tools to not only identify potential fraud but also to understand its underlying mechanisms.

The application of NLP in fraud detection transcends traditional methods, offering a dynamic and proactive approach to safeguarding assets and reputation. By automating the analysis of vast datasets, identifying patterns, and decoding linguistic subtleties, NLP provides a robust layer of defense against the ingenious tactics of fraudsters. Furthermore, its adaptability in the face of new challenges like deepfakes and AI-generated content underscores its potential as a versatile and indispensable tool in the arsenal against fraud.

However, as we embrace the power of NLP in combating fraud, it is imperative to tread with ethical diligence, balancing vigilance with respect for privacy and data protection. The journey ahead is not without challenges, but with continuous advancements in NLP technology and a strategic approach to its implementation, businesses can fortify their defenses against fraud. Embracing NLP is not just about deploying a new technology; it's about committing to a culture of innovation, vigilance, and ethical responsibility.

As we look to the future, it is clear that NLP will continue to play a pivotal role in the shaping of fraud detection. Its integration into business operations will evolve, becoming more sophisticated and intuitive. For businesses, staying abreast of these advancements and integrating NLP into their fraud detection strategies will be key to staying one step ahead of fraudsters. In this digital age, where fraudsters constantly seek new avenues to exploit, machine learning offers hope and is a powerful tool for ensuring security, integrity, and trust in the business world.

Chapter 8
From Chaos to Order: Organizing Information

In Chapter 8, we will look at the modern-day challenges of information overload that confront us. Today, we are constantly bombarded with information from various digital sources. From emails and social media feeds to news articles and research papers, the amount of content we encounter on a daily basis can be overwhelming. The digital era, while bringing a wealth of information at our fingertips, also presents the Herculean task of organizing this vast reservoir of data into a structured and comprehensible form. As we venture into this chapter, we explore the challenge of information overload and how Natural Language Processing can emerge as a leader of order amidst a sea of chaotic data. Through the lens of NLP, we will traverse the journey from chaos to order, unveiling the methodologies that can help us organize and make sense of the boundless information that envelop us.

Today, we live in a world where information is abundant and easily accessible. While this has its advantages, it also presents a challenge - information overload. We are constantly bombarded with a never-ending stream of emails, notifications, and news articles. This can make it difficult to filter out the relevant information and can lead to feelings of overwhelm and cognitive overload.

To overcome this challenge, we can leverage the power of Natural Language Processing to automatically categorize and tag information. NLP algorithms can analyze the content of emails, articles, and other forms of information and assign them relevant labels or tags, making it easier to search and organize. By implementing NLP-based information filtering systems, we can prioritize and access the information that is most relevant to us, thereby saving time and mental energy.

How can Natural Language Processing be utilized to manage and personalize the vast influx of information in our digital environment?

Fortunately, NLP offers a range of solutions to help us filter through the overwhelming amount of information. NLP algorithms can be used to automatically categorize and tag information, making it easier to find and organize. By leveraging NLP techniques, we can create personalized filters that prioritize the information that is most relevant to us, saving time and mental energy.

The first step in implementing NLP-based information filtering systems is to train the algorithms to recognize patterns and characteristics that are associated with our preferences. This can be done by providing the algorithms with labeled examples of information that we find relevant or irrelevant. The algorithms can then use this labeled data to learn the patterns and characteristics that distinguish relevant from irrelevant information.

Once the algorithms have been trained, they can be applied to new incoming information to automatically categorize and tag it. This can be done based on various factors, such as topic, source, author, or keywords. By leveraging NLP for information filtering, we can create personalized information feeds that prioritize the content that is most important to us, while filtering out noise and irrelevant information.

Another challenge we face with information overload is the sheer length of the content we encounter. Reading long articles or reports can be time-consuming, especially when we are short on time. NLP can come to the rescue by providing solutions for automatic summarization. NLP algorithms can extract the key points and main ideas from a piece of text, condensing it into a concise summary that captures the essence of the content.

To achieve this, NLP algorithms analyze the structure and content of the text and identify the most salient information. This can include important sentences, phrases, or key concepts. The algorithms can then generate a summary that highlights these key points, giving readers a quick overview of the content without having to read the entire text.

Automatic summarization can be applied to various types of content, such as news articles, research papers, or even emails. By summarizing information, NLP not only saves us time but also helps us to prioritize and focus on the most important information.

Once we have filtered and summarized the information, the next step is to organize it in a way that is easily accessible and manageable. NLP techniques can be used to create intelligent knowledge bases or document repositories. By analyzing the content and extracting relevant information, NLP algorithms can automatically tag and categorize documents, making it easier to search and retrieve information when needed.

To organize information effectively, NLP algorithms use a combination of techniques such as text classification, named entity recognition, and topic modeling. These techniques enable the algorithms to understand the content of documents and assign them relevant tags or categories. This allows us to search for information based on specific criteria, such as topic, date, or author.

In addition to organizing information based on predefined categories, NLP can also identify relationships and connections between different pieces of information. This can be done through techniques such as entity linking or co-occurrence analysis. By understanding the relationships between information, NLP algorithms can provide additional context and make it easier to explore related topics or concepts.

In addition to organizing information, NLP can also provide personalized recommendations based on our preferences and interests. By analyzing our past behavior and interactions with content, NLP algorithms can suggest articles, books, or other resources that are likely to be of interest to us. This not only saves time in searching for relevant information but also helps us discover new topics or perspectives.

NLP-powered recommendation systems analyze various factors to generate personalized recommendations. These factors can include our browsing history, social media interactions, or even our personal preferences and interests. By understanding these factors, NLP algorithms can make informed predictions about the type of content that is likely to resonate with us.

To provide accurate and relevant recommendations, NLP algorithms use techniques such as collaborative filtering, content-based filtering, or hybrid approaches. These techniques enable the algorithms to identify patterns and similarities between different pieces of content and make recommendations based on those patterns.

In today's globalized world, the ability to organize information in multiple languages is becoming increasingly important. NLP techniques can be used to process and analyze text in different languages, enabling us to organize and search for information across language barriers. This opens up new opportunities for collaboration and knowledge sharing in multilingual contexts.

To organize multilingual information effectively, NLP algorithms need to be able to understand and process text in different languages. This can be achieved through techniques such as machine translation or cross-lingual information retrieval. By leveraging these techniques, NLP algorithms can bridge the language gap and enable us to access information in languages that we may not be proficient in.

Cross-language information organization also involves addressing challenges such as language-specific nuances, cultural differences, or the availability of language resources. NLP algorithms need to be trained and tested on multilingual data to ensure their effectiveness in organizing and searching for information in different languages.

How can we use NLP for fact checking and information verification?

In an era of fake news and misinformation, verifying the accuracy of information is crucial. NLP can assist in fact-checking by analyzing the content for credibility and verifiability. NLP algorithms can compare the information against trusted sources, detect inconsistencies or biases, and provide insights into the reliability of the content.

To fact-check and verify information, NLP algorithms use techniques such as information extraction, knowledge graph construction, or entity linking. These techniques enable the algorithms to compare information against a knowledge base of known facts and identify potential inconsistencies or falsehoods.

NLP algorithms can also analyze the linguistic features and patterns in the content to detect misleading or biased information. By understanding the context and the language used, NLP algorithms can provide insights into the reliability and trustworthiness of the information.

Again, we will look at NLP-powered chatbots and how they can be a valuable tool in information organization. By interacting with chatbots, we can ask questions, search for specific information, or request recommendations. NLP algorithms enable chatbots to understand and interpret natural language, providing us with instant access to relevant information in a conversational manner.

Chatbots can be integrated with existing information systems or knowledge bases, making it easier to search and retrieve information. Through natural language understanding and generation, NLP-powered chatbots extract meaning from user queries and provide relevant responses. This enhances the accessibility and usability of the information, as we can interact with chatbots in a conversational and intuitive manner.

Additionally, chatbots can learn from user interactions, allowing them to improve their understanding and accuracy over time. By leveraging machine learning techniques, chatbots can adapt to user preferences and provide personalized recommendations or responses.

While NLP offers powerful solutions for information organization, it is essential to consider ethical implications. Protecting user privacy, ensuring data security, and addressing potential biases are critical factors in the responsible use of NLP for information organization. Striking a balance between convenience and ethical considerations is crucial for establishing trust and maintaining the integrity of the information ecosystem.

When organizing information with NLP, it is important to prioritize user privacy and ensure that sensitive information is handled securely. NLP algorithms should comply with privacy regulations and provide users with transparent control over their data. Additionally, steps should be taken to minimize bias in information organization, as NLP algorithms can inadvertently perpetuate existing biases present in the data.

Moreover, ethical considerations in NLP-based information organization include ensuring transparency in how the algorithms operate, being accountable for the decisions made based on the algorithms' output, and continuously monitoring and evaluating the performance and impact of the algorithms.

As technology continues to evolve, so does the field of information organization. NLP will play a crucial role in shaping the future of how we organize and access information. Emerging trends such as knowledge graphs, semantic search, and context-aware recommendation systems offer exciting possibilities for enhancing our information organization capabilities.

Knowledge graphs, for example, provide a structured way of representing and organizing information, enabling more intelligent search and retrieval. Semantic search, on the other hand, focuses on understanding the meaning and intent behind user queries, allowing for more accurate and relevant results. Context-aware recommendation systems leverage NLP to personalize recommendations based on factors such as time, location, or user preferences, enhancing the user experience.

Concluding this chapter on managing information overload today underscores the critical role of technology in language processing in reshaping our approach to data. Amidst the flood of digital content, this technology empowers us to not only cope but excel in the vast amount of information today. By facilitating automatic categorization, summarization, and organization of data, it provides essential tools for navigating and comprehending the immense stream of information we face every day.

The chapter has outlined how NLP-powered systems can transform chaotic streams of data into structured, comprehensible, and actionable insights. We delved into how these systems can automate the filtering of irrelevant data, summarize extensive content, and organize information in a way that enhances accessibility and comprehension. The use of NLP in fact-checking and information verification, particularly in the era of misinformation, highlights its critical role in ensuring the credibility and reliability of the data we consume.

Moreover, NLP's potential in facilitating multilingual information processing and personalized content recommendations was discussed, underscoring its capacity to adapt to the evolving needs of a diverse, global audience. The integration of NLP into chatbots and virtual assistants was also explored, showcasing how these technologies can streamline our interactions with information in a more intuitive and conversational manner.

However, as we embrace these advancements, the chapter also cautions us about the ethical considerations in employing NLP. The need to balance efficiency with privacy, security, and fairness is paramount. As we harness NLP's capabilities, we must remain vigilant about data protection, address biases in algorithms, and ensure transparency in information processing.

Looking forward, the chapter suggests that the role of NLP in information organization will continue to grow and evolve. Emerging technologies like knowledge graphs, semantic search, and context-aware systems promise to further enhance our ability to navigate and make sense of the vast digital world we know now.

Chapter 9

Personal Virtual Assistants: Elevating Daily Tasks

In the whirlwind of today's rapid-fire life, the allure of personal virtual assistants (PVAs) isn't just a luxury—it's an unyielding necessity. As the heartbeats of our digital existence, these assistants, powered by revolutionary natural language processing, are redefining the essence of everyday life. They are our modern-day digital companions, tirelessly orchestrating a symphony of tasks, carving out seamless operations from the cacophony of our daily engagements.

This chapter is your gateway to the dynamic universe where virtual assistants morph mundane tasks into exhilarating experiences, where every interaction is not just a transaction, but a step towards a more streamlined, efficient, and engaging reality. As we unravel the saga of their evolution, you'll witness the dawn of a new era of productivity, the magic of personalized recommendations forging a path of effortless decisions, the eloquence of seamless communication, and the mastery in schedule management.

Venture further and discover how the secure vaults of information, the smart home integration, the ease of travel facilitation, and the inspiring fitness assistance are not mere concepts, but tangible realities enhancing the quality of life. And amidst this exciting journey, we'll also tread on the grounds of ethics, ensuring that the bright flame of innovation shines within the defined boundaries of right and just. The chapters ahead are more than just pages; they are the windows to a captivating reality sculpted by NLP, through the lens of personal virtual assistants, a reality that's not in the distant future, but at the cusp of today!

Personal virtual assistants is a remarkable technology that many businesses and individuals use today, and thus represent a remarkable chapter. Originating from the rudimentary voice recognition systems, they have burgeoned into sophisticated companions, tirelessly adapting and learning from user interactions. The crescendo of this evolution resonates with the harmonics of Natural Language Processing, a technology that empowers these digital allies to transcend traditional interaction paradigms, laying the foundation for unprecedented convenience.

The journey commenced with humble attempts at recognizing and interpreting human speech. Yet, with every stride along the timeline, NLP endowed PVAs with a deeper comprehension of language, enabling a more organic, intuitive interaction between humans and machines. Today, the synergy between Artificial Intelligence and Voice User Interface (VUI) technologies has catalyzed a transformative wave, morphing PVAs from mere voice-activated tools into insightful, proactive allies.

As we glance towards the horizon, the promise of a future where PVAs handle complex tasks and interactions isn't a distant dream but an impending reality. These virtual companions, fueled by ceaseless advancements in Artificial Intelligence and NLP, are on the cusp of revolutionizing the way we interact with the digital realm. Personal virtual assistance isn't one of stagnation but of relentless innovation. They are no longer confined to the simplistic task of recognizing voice commands; they now engage in meaningful conversations, learn from past interactions, and even anticipate user needs, embodying a blend of technological innovation and personalized assistance.

The tapestry of PVA evolution reflects not merely a technological shift but a societal one. It's a testament to how deeply integrated digital companions have become in our daily lives, shaping routines, refining interactions, and emboldening a generation to envision a future where the alliance between humans and machines pioneers a new epoch of convenience and efficiency.

The illustrious domain of personal virtual assistants shines its brightest when steering the ship of productivity amidst the tumultuous sea of tasks that beckon our attention daily. The essence of these assistants lies in their prowess to morph the chaos of daily chores into a symphony of organized tasks. They stand as vigilant sentinels, ensuring no meeting is missed, no birthday forgotten, and no task overlooked. Setting up a meeting, crafting a shopping list, or sending out timely reminders, these assistants exhibit a distinguished level of mastery in managing time and tasks. The secret to their proficient execution? The pioneering algorithms of Natural Language Processing that empower them.

NLP, with its remarkable capability to understand, interpret, and generate human language, endows these assistants with the discernment to sift through the haystack of tasks and pinpoint the needles of priority. The mundane routine, often seen as an unending treadmill, is transformed into a strategic game of chess where every move is calculated and every task is accorded its rightful place. The fast growing, relentless pace of today's lifestyle demands a proactive approach to task management, an approach that virtual assistants, backed by NLP's advanced algorithms, provide with unparalleled expertise.

The innovation does not stop at merely organizing tasks. The horizon extends to offering valuable insights that enable better management of tasks, thereby revolutionizing the traditional paradigms of productivity. By analyzing past behaviors, preferences, and routines, these assistants not only manage tasks but also offer suggestions to optimize time and efforts. The game-changer here is the elimination of stress from mundane routines, offering a breath of fresh air to individuals engulfed in the daily grind.

The transformative impact resonates beyond individual benefits to creating a ripple effect across the professional ecosystem. By automating repetitive tasks, these virtual assistants free up valuable time, which can then be channeled towards more strategic, impactful endeavors. This ripple grows into a wave of increased efficiency and productivity, setting a new benchmark in task management. The legacy of virtual assistants in enhancing productivity is a testament to the resilient and agile nature of NLP, a field that continues to evolve and adapt to the exigencies of modern life. As we continue to thrive in the digital age, the synergy between virtual assistants and NLP stands as a luminary trailblazer, leading the charge towards a more organized, efficient, and productive reality.

We now see more personal virtual assistants and see the impact they are making as luminary guides in the expedition of discovering resonating content in the media and entertainment industry. The prowess of natural language processing underpins this bespoke journey, fostering a rich, tailored experience that mirrors individual preferences and behaviors. The joy of stumbling upon a stirring piece of music, an invigorating article, or an enthralling movie is an unmatched pleasure. These intelligent companions, with their adept algorithms, curate a unique palette of suggestions that resonate with your taste, effortlessly bridging the gap between the vast ocean of content and your preferences.

Engaging with a personal virtual assistant is akin to having a dedicated companion by your side, one that understands your taste with remarkable expertise. As you voice your desire to explore new music or read about recent happenings, your digital companion sifts through the overwhelming sea of information, picking out the pearls that align with your interests. The methodology is not merely about matching keywords but understanding the essence of your preferences, analyzing past behaviors to project thought into what might spark your interest next.

The ability to have personalized recommendations is a fast-growing frontier, reflecting a transformative shift from generic to personalized, from being lost in the crowd to having a spotlight on your unique preferences. The paradigm here is not just about the convenience of finding resonating content but about creating a fluid environment where discovery is a joy, not a chore. This transformation is a game-changer in how we interact with the digital world, making the engagement a reflection of our unique tastes and preferences.

The exponential impact of this personalization is far-reaching. It's about saving time, reducing the inconvenience of wading through irrelevant content, and most importantly, making the digital engagement an exhilarating experience. This era of personalization heralded by NLP is not just a trend but a robust framework that is set to redefine the contours of digital engagement in the media and entertainment sector.

Virtual assistants armed with NLP algorithms, stand as the epitome of effortless communication and collaboration. They are the invisible threads weaving through the fabric of our digital interactions, ensuring seamless connectivity across various channels. The integration with email, calendar, and messaging apps is more than just a feature; it's a revolutionary step towards fostering a culture of effortless communication and collaboration.

The objective here is not about replacing human interaction but augmenting it to a level of ease and efficiency that was previously unattainable. Whether it's about sending a quick message through voice commands, scheduling meetings without the to-and-fro of emails, or making calls, NLP-powered assistants are the agile facilitators in this dance of digital interactions. The brilliance of NLP lies in its ability to understand and process natural language, turning a voice command into an action, an intent into a scheduled meeting, a thought into a communicated message.

The strategic integration of NLP with virtual assistants has unveiled a new era where communication is not a hurdle but a catalyst for effective collaboration. The pioneering spirit of NLP has morphed the mundane task of scheduling, communicating, and collaborating into an engaging, efficient, and seamless experience. The synergy between NLP algorithms and virtual assistants' capabilities is a bold step towards redefining the norms of digital communication.

It is a known notation in todays business world that time is scarce, an invaluable asset. The quest for effective time management often feels like navigating through a complex labyrinth. Here, personal virtual assistants, empowered by the magic of Natural Language Processing, become the compass, guiding through the maze of schedules and commitments. Their prowess lies in automating the intricacies of schedule management, morphing a hectic day into a well-orchestrated symphony of events.

The virtual assistant becomes the guardian of time, meticulously keeping track of appointments, deadlines, and important dates. Yet, its service transcends mere tracking. By offering proactive reminders, it ensures commitments are honored, fostering a culture of punctuality and accountability. Each reminder is a gentle nudge, a courteous whisper amidst the cacophony of daily tasks, ensuring important events do not fall through the cracks.

Furthermore, the virtual assistant evolves into a wise counselor for better time management. By analyzing past schedules and current commitments, it offers insightful suggestions for a balanced life. Perhaps, a reshuffling of meetings to avoid rush hours, or spreading out deadlines to prevent burnout. The recommendations are tailored, aiming to weave a fine balance between professional commitments and personal leisure.

The journey towards effective time management is no longer solitary. The virtual assistant, with its NLP-powered understanding, emerges as a reliable companion. The experience is akin to having a personal secretary, one that holds a mirror to time, reflecting the opportunities to optimize and thrive.

As we look at personal virtual assistants, its important to think about data that is transmitted through them, whether they are software or a real human who is remote. Data is both an asset and a vulnerability, the safeguarding of personal information becomes paramount. The NLP-powered virtual assistants emerge as vigilant sentinels guarding the fortress of personal data. They embody a blend of smart storage solutions and robust security measures, ensuring the sanctity of sensitive information.

The fortress is impenetrable, with advanced encryption techniques forming the robust walls against unauthorized access. Yet, for the rightful owner, access is but a voice command away. The virtual assistant, with voice authentication, ensures that data access is both secure and convenient. The methodology here is about creating a seamless blend of security and accessibility.

Moreover, the intelligent management extends to how personal data is organized and retrieved. Through voice commands, a query plunges into the depths of stored data, fetching the required information with agility and accuracy. This is not just about security, but smart management, where data is not a jumbled maze but a well-organized, easily navigable repository.

Personal information management and security is about restoring control and peace of mind in the digital interactions. The NLP-powered virtual assistants are not just tools but trusted allies in preserving, managing, and accessing personal data. Through innovative security measures and smart data management solutions, they exemplify a significant stride towards a secure, organized digital existence.

Home is in every essance a sanctuary of comfort and convenience. In this serene space, virtual assistants emerge as the maestros orchestrating a symphony of smart home devices. The magic unfolds with a mere utterance, turning the abode into a haven where lights, music, and climate dance to the tune of voice commands.

The core of this magic lies in the seamless integration with smart home devices. Whether it's illuminating the rooms with the soft glow of lights, setting the thermostat to cradle in a warm embrace, or filling the halls with melodious tunes, the virtual assistant makes it happen with an effortless ease. The experience is like having an invisible genie, awaiting to fulfill every wish, creating a contained environment tailored to personal preferences.

But the service extends beyond mere obedience to commands. The virtual assistants, with their NLP prowess, learn, adapt, and even anticipate the needs. They analyze habitual preferences, like the preferred room temperature or the favored playlist during dinner, and automatically adjust the settings. The home thus morphs into a living entity, resonating with the inhabitants' preferences, embodying comfort and convenience at every corner.

Moreover, smart home integration is a leap towards sustainable living. By optimizing energy usage, like dimming lights in unoccupied rooms or regulating thermostat based on weather forecasts, virtual assistants contribute to energy conservation. This is smart living in a true sense, where comfort meets sustainability, steered by the ingenious integration of virtual assistants with smart home devices.

The thought of travel often comes with a blend of excitement and challenges. Here, virtual assistants morph into personal travel concierges, smoothing out the wrinkles in travel plans. Powered by NLP algorithms, they become the bridge to a myriad of travel-related services, making bookings, fetching real-time updates, or even discovering gastronomic delights in uncharted cities.

At the outset, booking tickets is a breeze. A simple voice command sets the wheels in motion, be it reserving a flight to a dream destination or booking a train to a quaint countryside. The virtual assistant handles the intricacies, leaving the adventurer to bask in the anticipation of the journey.

But the assistant's role doesn't end with bookings. They stand as vigilant sentinels monitoring flight schedules, alerting the traveler about any delays or changes. In unknown cities, they morph into personal guides, suggesting the finest restaurants or the hidden gems tucked away from the usual tourist trails.

Moreover, they assist in navigating through the streets, making every journey an expedition of discovery rather than a test of patience. The road less traveled is no longer a path of uncertainty but an avenue of exploration, thanks to the insightful guidance of virtual assistants.

In essence, virtual assistants turn travel from a task of meticulous planning into an endeavor of effortless exploration. They handle the mundane, leaving the traveler to soak in the experiences, making each journey not just a travel but a tale worth telling.

Today's, virtual assistants emerge as proactive companions on this quest. They transcend from being mere digital entities to personalized fitness coaches, each interaction tailored to the unique wellness goals of the individual.

Unveiling the era of personalized workout sessions, virtual assistants craft workout regimens that resonate with personal fitness levels and aspirations. They provide a seamless blend of cardio drills, strength training, and mindfulness practices, ensuring a holistic approach to fitness. With the prowess of NLP, they interpret feedback, adapt routines, and ensure the fitness journey remains engaging and impactful.

The journey towards optimal health is not just about physical exertion; it's a lifestyle. Here, virtual assistants provide invaluable support by offering personalized diet tips. They analyze dietary preferences, nutritional needs, and even the local market's offerings to provide recommendations that are both nourishing and accessible. The aim is to foster a sustainable dietary habit that aligns with the health goals yet satiates the palate.

Amidst the hustle of daily chores, taking breaks is often overlooked. Virtual assistants serve as gentle reminders to pause, breathe, and rejuvenate. They ensure that the individual steps away from the grind, indulges in a moment of relaxation or a short walk, and returns with renewed vigor.

Monitoring activities is the cornerstone of progressing on the fitness path. Virtual assistants keep a vigilant eye on daily physical activities, sleep quality, and even mental wellness. They provide insightful feedback, celebrate milestones, and keep the motivation soaring. The goal is to nurture a supportive environment that propels one towards a healthier lifestyle.

Personal virtual assistants serve as a bridge between humans and the boundless digital cosmos in our highly digital lives we live today. They heed our commands, answer our queries, and strive to make life a tad easier. However, as they weave into the fabric of daily life, they bring along a basket of ethical considerations. At the heart of these considerations lie three pivotal elements: user privacy, data protection, and informed consent.

User privacy unfolds as virtual assistants collect, store, and analyze heaps of personal data. Every query, every command funnels through the digital veins of these assistants, painting a vivid picture of the user's life. This amassed data could serve as a treasure trove for personalized services, yet also a potential goldmine for nefarious purposes. The balance between harnessing data for personalization and safeguarding privacy is a tightrope that demands delicate tread.

Segueing into data protection, the discourse intensifies. The guardianship of sensitive data is a mantle of immense responsibility. Advanced encryption and robust security measures are the shields against the onslaught of data breaches and cyber-attacks. Yet, the arms race between security protocols and hacking ingenuity is relentless. The onus is on creating an impenetrable fortress safeguarding the user data, a task demanding ceaseless vigilance and innovation.

Informed consent is the third vertex of this ethical triangle. It's the user's unequivocal nod to the collection and usage of their data. However, the intricacies of what consents are granted, often lurk in the shadows of lengthy, complex terms of service agreements. The essence of informed consent is rooted in clarity and understanding, empowering users with the knowledge of how their data is utilized and protected.

Engaging in a profound dialogue encompassing these ethical considerations is not a choice but a necessity. The discourse should resonate in the halls of regulatory bodies, echo within the walls of corporations, and find a voice among the user community. Ethical considerations should not be mere footnotes but pivotal chapters we consider when talking about personal virtual assistant usage.

Moreover, the visionary approach would be to embed ethics into the DNA of virtual assistant technology. Ethical considerations should guide the design, development, and deployment phases, ensuring a robust framework that respects privacy, guarantees data protection, and upholds informed consent.

The journey of personal virtual assistants from being a novelty to a necessity has been swift and impactful. Yet, as they entrench deeper into the daily routines, the ethical canvas upon which they operate needs meticulous crafting. It's a collective endeavor, demanding the synergy of technologists, policymakers, and users. An endeavor, that's not just about navigating the ethical maze but mastering it, ensuring that as virtual assistants augment our lives, they honor the ethical principles that are the bedrock of trust and confidence.

As we steer through the history of Personal Virtual Assistants (PVAs), their significant impact on our daily lives is undeniable. They have not only simplified complex tasks but also shaped a future where seamless interaction with the digital world is a tangible reality. Our exploration of PVAs reveals their profound influence on our daily routines, productivity, and the very nature of our homes. They have expanded the realms of possibility, turning everyday tasks into something extraordinary.

It's crucial to acknowledge the deep ethical considerations intertwined with the use of PVAs. This calls for a deeper discourse to ensure that, as we advance into a future filled with technological wonders, we remain grounded in the principles that sustain the fabric of society. The discussion around user privacy, data protection, and informed consent is not a mere sideline but a necessary route to be traversed with awareness and responsibility.

Looking at the profound synergy between Artificial Intelligence, Natural Language Processing, and the world of PVAs, we are observing not just a technological revolution but a societal transformation. It's a shift towards a future where our digital companions become extensions of our wishes, mirrors of our preferences, and guardians of our private information.

The relentless wave of innovation propels PVAs to realms once considered science fiction. Yet, here we are, at the cusp of a reality where your voice echoes through smart homes, where personalized advice is a voice command away, where managing the chaos of daily life is a simplified affair. And while we revel in these conveniences, the dialogue around the ethical footprint of these innovations is a compass guiding us through the unchartered waters.

The widespread use of PVAs is a testament to human ingenuity, a wellspring of creativity that is ceaselessly pushing the boundaries of what's possible. As we stand on the threshold of a future punctuated by the harmonious symphony between humans and virtual assistants, it's not just an ode to innovation but a call to responsible advancement. The chapters traversed have not only showcased the marvels of PVAs but have also beckoned us to envision a future where technology and humanity prosper together, bound by ethics, thriving on innovation, and flourishing in mutual respect and understanding.

Chapter 10
Lifelong Learning: NLP in Education

In this invigorating chapter, we will talk about the transformative ability of Natural Language Processing as it intricately stacks the building blocks of education and lifelong learning. A spectrum of innovative applications, from the realms of intelligent tutoring systems to the pioneering domain of automated skill assessment. NLP, with its profound ability to interpret and generate human language, emerges as a luminary force, meticulously carving a new epoch in the way we acquire knowledge, enhance learning outcomes, and resiliently adapt to the demands of a rapidly metamorphosing world.

We will uncover the remarkable ways in which it is reshaping the contours of learning. We will start with a look into intelligent tutoring systems, where NLP serves as the backbone, orchestrating a personalized learning environment that resonates with the unique cognitive and learning styles of each individual. We will see how these systems, empowered by NLP, foster a nurturing environment that meticulously identifies the strengths, weaknesses, and the unique learning pace of every learner, thereby crafting a tailored learning pathway that not only enhances comprehension but ignites the spark of curiosity and the joy of discovery.

Segueing into automated skill assessments, the chapter will look at how NLP stands as a linchpin in revolutionizing the evaluation paradigm. Through the lens of NLP, we witness a shift from the traditional assessment models to a more nuanced, personalized assessment framework that understands the learner's proficiency, adapts to their learning trajectory, and provides insightful feedback that catalyzes growth and mastery of skills.

Moreover, as we look further, we will explore how natural language processing is a catalyst in democratizing education, breaking down geographical and linguistic barriers, thereby fostering a global learning community. The chapter highlights the unprecedented opportunities NLP offers in creating interactive, engaging, and accessible learning experiences, regardless of the learner's location or linguistic background.

As we continue in this compelling chapter, we illuminate how Natural Language Processing is not just a technological breakthrough, but a source of inspiration in fostering a culture of continuous learning. It invites us to imagine an educational environment that is more inclusive, interactive, and filled with endless opportunities that arise when technology and education blend seamlessly. Through the perspective of this technology, we are encouraged to envision a future where learning is personalized, engaging, and enriching, a path that cultivates a culture of constant curiosity, discovery, and expertise.

Venturing into the field of education, we observe how Natural Language Processing acts as a catalyst in enhancing the creation and delivery of educational content. With the prowess of NLP, educators and content creators have the tools to improve comprehension through automatic text summarization and simplification. The algorithms intrinsic to NLP analyze complex texts, generating succinct summaries or rewriting them in a more accessible language. This not only aids in breaking down complex concepts into digestible bits but also paves the way for more engaging learning material.

Natural language processing stands as a forerunner in supporting personalized learning experiences. Through adaptive content recommendations based on individual learning preferences and proficiency levels, NLP creates a fluid environment for learners. Each recommendation is tailored, addressing the unique learning curve of every individual, thereby fostering a thriving learning atmosphere.

Furthermore, Natural Language Processing extends to the creation of interactive educational resources that resonate with each learner's pace and comprehension, fostering a harmonious educational experience. Through this technology, we envision a future where educational materials are not static texts, but dynamic resources that interact, adapt, and evolve with the learner.

Personalized instruction is undergoing a revolution with the advent of Intelligent Tutoring Systems empowered by this technology. These systems, equipped to analyze learner data, provide customized feedback and guidance, catering to individual learning needs with remarkable precision.

These systems meticulously analyze student responses and interactions, pinpointing areas for improvement and adjusting instructional strategies to enhance learning outcomes. This personalized approach not only bolsters the effectiveness of instruction but also makes the learning experience more engaging and interactive.

The feedback provided by these systems is insightful, enabling learners to understand their progress and focus on areas needing more attention. This synergy between this technology and Intelligent Tutoring Systems is pioneering a new paradigm in education, transforming learning into a more insightful, engaging, and customized journey.

Additionally, we observe how this technology is revolutionizing automated skill assessments. Algorithms adeptly analyze written or spoken responses from learners, enabling the evaluation of knowledge and proficiency across various subjects with remarkable accuracy. This innovative approach marks a significant advancement in educational methods.

The core of automated assessment lies in its ability to streamline evaluations, providing timely and insightful feedback to learners. This aspect of the technology delves deeper than just identifying right or wrong answers. By analyzing patterns in incorrect responses, it uncovers underlying misconceptions or gaps in knowledge, offering valuable insights for educators to provide targeted support and craft more effective learning pathways.

Moreover, this technology's role in education goes beyond assessment. It signifies a paradigm shift, making the learning process more transparent, guided, and enriched with insights. Learners become active participants in a tailored educational experience, where their unique needs and learning styles are recognized and catered to. This strategic, learner-centric approach is set to empower, innovate, and create a learning environment that is both adaptable and inspirational.

Transitioning to language learning, the integration of this technology into applications is transformative. Automated translation, a standout feature, allows learners to effortlessly access content in multiple languages, dismantling language barriers and fostering a prolific learning environment. The technology excels in speech recognition and pronunciation analysis, offering a platform for learners to refine their spoken language skills. These applications provide constructive feedback, emulating the expertise of a seasoned language instructor.

Language proficiency assessment tools, powered by this technology, offer objective and accurate evaluations, essential for learners to track their progress. Through a seamless interface, learners receive real-time feedback, accelerating the learning curve and ensuring a progressive language learning journey.

Personalized language instruction also finds a robust expression through this technology. Tailored to individual needs and learning styles, it optimizes the language acquisition process. Each learner's journey is unique, and this technology stands out in recognizing and adapting to these distinct learning curves.

This technology also unveils possibilities for supporting students with special educational needs. Text-to-speech and speech recognition technologies are instrumental for students with disabilities, aiding in communication tasks and ensuring full participation in classroom activities. These technologies simplify the communication challenge, ensuring an inclusive educational environment.

Adaptive learning environments, underpinned by NLP algorithms, provide personalized instruction and support. This adaptation accommodates individual learning styles and pace, ensuring every learner finds a rhythm that resonates with their capabilities. The methodology employed is nuanced, providing a scalable solution that adapts to the diverse needs within special education.

Moreover, NLP sentiment analysis is a remarkable innovation, helping to identify and address emotional hurdles that may impact learning. This analysis is instrumental in promoting a positive and inclusive learning atmosphere. By monitoring and understanding the emotional undertones in student communication, educators are empowered to create a supportive environment, addressing concerns that transcend mere academic challenges.

Through these myriad applications, NLP is pioneering a new epoch in special education. The strategic integration of NLP in educational methodologies is not only innovative but also a reflection of how technology can be harnessed to foster a more inclusive and adaptive learning environment.

In today's educational spheres, the role of Natural Language Processing in enhancing collaborative learning environments is becoming increasingly tenacious. The synergy between collaboration and knowledge sharing finds a prolific ally in NLP-powered tools. The core of this alliance lies in the capacity of Natural Language Understanding to significantly enhance communication and comprehension within a group dynamic, creating a fluid environment conducive to knowledge exchange.

One of the revolutionary aspects of NLP is sentiment analysis which acts as a luminary in gauging the emotional state of learners. By identifying potential emotional barriers, it provides a pathway to address these aspects, thus creating a supportive and inclusive learning atmosphere. This is a cornerstone in promoting an engaging collaborative learning environment where knowledge exchange flourishes.

In such environments, the role of educators transcends to become facilitators, empowering students to thrive in a collaborative setting. The transparency in communication, fostered by NLP, paves the way for effective knowledge sharing and problem-solving, hallmark of a prosperous collaborative learning environment.

Pedagogical research, leading the way in educational innovation, significantly benefits from the integration of natural language processing techniques. These tools are not merely supportive but transformative in analyzing and deriving insights from educational data. Text mining and sentiment analysis stand as remarkable tools enabling researchers to dissect student feedback and engagement, thus providing a deeper understanding of teaching effectiveness and student experiences.

Moreover, the ability of NLP algorithms to sift through large educational datasets to identify trends and patterns is a game-changer. This methodology of unearthing evidence-based practices is instrumental in informing pedagogical decisions. Optimizing teaching strategies and improving learning outcomes finds a bold expression through the leverage of NLP.

In this vein, the drive towards continuous improvement in teaching strategies embarks on a strategic route. By harnessing the potential of NLP, educators and researchers are not only able to adapt to the needs and preferences of students but also pioneer in providing a rich, engaging, and effective learning experience. The journey of pedagogical research, empowered by NLP, is on a trajectory towards creating a legacy of excellence in educational practices.

Natural language processing's role in educational data analytics as equally transformative. By employing NLP in educational data analysis, educators unlock a treasure trove of insights from vast educational datasets. Key techniques like text mining and sentiment analysis become instrumental in uncovering learner emotions and attitudes. This thorough understanding is crucial, as it allows educators to pinpoint specific areas that either ignite student interest or signal potential concerns, enabling them to craft more effective and personalized educational interventions. Harnessing the potential of Natural Language Processing in educational data analytics paves the way for extracting invaluable insights from educational data. At the forefront, text mining and sentiment analysis emerge as luminary tools enabling the deciphering of learner emotions and attitudes towards learning. This understanding is pivotal, as it empowers educators to identify areas sparking interest or concern, thereby tailoring interventions accordingly.

NLP's prowess extends to predictive modeling and clustering techniques, thus facilitating the prediction of student success. Through meticulous analysis of historical data patterns, NLP identifies students at the brink of academic difficulties. This proactive approach is a game-changer, as it fosters a supportive learning environment where timely interventions can be deployed.

We can optimize interventions and support, tailored to individual student needs, finding a bold expression through NLP. By leveraging this disruptive technology, educators are empowered to craft a learning environment that is both engaging and conducive to academic success. The tailored interventions are a testament to how NLP can be harnessed to foster a culture of continuous improvement and personalized learning.

Engaging with NLP in educational settings brings to the forefront a myriad of ethical considerations. Ensuring student privacy and data protection is paramount, given the sensitive nature of educational data. Implementing robust security measures and complying with privacy regulations arc non-negotiables to uphold trust and confidence in the use of NLP in educational arenas.

The discussion of balancing personalized learning with ethical considerations regarding data usage is both crucial and ongoing. This conversation provides a platform to reflect on and ensure the responsible and ethical application of Natural Language Processing in education. An open exchange among industry leaders, educators, and policymakers is vital to address ethical concerns, aiming for a harmonious balance between personalized learning and data privacy.

The exploration of ethical issues serves as a reminder of the responsibility that comes with using this technology in education. Careful thought and proactive discussions are fundamental in ensuring that its integration in educational settings is ethical and beneficial for everyone involved. By focusing on these ethical aspects, the advancement of this technology in education can flourish, bringing unparalleled benefits while maintaining the highest standards of ethical practice.

Looking at the current educational horizon, it's aglow with the potential of groundbreaking innovations brought by this technology. Its capacity to transform the educational experience is vast and thrilling. With rapid advancements in this technology, we witness the rise of conversational agents and augmented reality, ushering in a new wave of innovative learning experiences and significantly boosting learner engagement.

Conversational agents exemplify the progress of this technology. Equipped to interact in a human-like manner, they are set to redefine educational dialogue. Offering a robust and interactive platform, these agents enable learners to participate in meaningful conversations, thereby enriching their educational experience.

Augmented reality (AR), meanwhile, is pioneering immersive educational environments. In conjunction with this technology, AR can create transformative and engaging learning experiences. The combination of AR and this technology facilitates an environment where learners can interact with educational content more intuitively and naturally.

Furthermore, the integration of NLP with other cutting-edge technologies such as Virtual Reality (VR) and adaptive learning platforms is a game-changer. It's a visionary approach that is creating immersive and personalized learning environments where learners can thrive. For instance, VR, when augmented with NLP, provides a contained environment where learners can interact with educational scenarios in a manner so authentic, it's revolutionary.

The journey does not end here. Adaptive learning platforms, empowered by NLP, are setting a new benchmark in personalized education. They cater to the individual learning preferences and pace, thus making learning a more tailored and enjoyable endeavor.

As NLP continues to innovate and evolve, the prospects of fostering lifelong learning and enabling individuals to adapt to future demands become more tangible. Natural language processing in education is one of continuous innovation and adaptation. It's about creating a legacy of educational excellence that is not only sustainable but also scalable.

The journey of NLP in education is filled with the promise of exponential growth and impactful advancements. The blend of NLP with emerging technologies is setting the stage for a prosperous and innovative educational future. It's a bold venture, one that holds the potential to redefine educational norms and set a new, inspiring precedent in how learning is approached and experienced.

In conclusion, the fusion of NLP with advancing technologies is not merely a trend but a strategic shift towards creating more engaging, effective, and personalized educational experiences. The future holds a promise of an education, where languiage processing is at the helm, steering the sector towards uncharted territories of excellence and innovation.

Chapter 11

Inclusive Technologies for Accessibility for All

In today's fast-paced technological world, Natural Language Processing stands to be an innovative force, particularly in the field of assistive technologies. we will explore how its integration into assistive devices represents more than just a technological achievement. It marks a significant step towards greater inclusivity and independence for individuals with motor, speech, and sensory impairments. Our focus is on understanding the crucial role this technology plays in transforming the interaction between technology and those it aims to support.

The incorporation of Natural Language Processing into assistive technologies represents a major leap forward for those with motor impairments. This integration is a response to the unique challenges faced by this community, reflecting a commitment to inclusivity and autonomy.

Voice-activated devices have revolutionized interactions for people with limited mobility. Evolving from basic command recognition to understanding nuanced instructions, these devices have broadened access to digital services like messaging and web browsing, all without physical contact.

The fusion of NLP with AI in smart assistants goes beyond obeying commands. These systems learn from user behavior, offering customized support that mirrors the attentiveness of human caregivers. They can handle intricate tasks via vocal instructions, symbolizing a significant stride in crafting adaptable environments for those with motor impairments.

Gesture-based control, merging with NLP, opens another dimension for interaction. Here, refined sensors translate subtle physical movements into digital commands, offering a novel way for individuals with mobility challenges to engage with technology.

This evolution in NLP application demonstrates a targeted and compassionate approach to tech development, where understanding the needs of motor-impaired individuals is as important as technological innovation. Collaborative efforts across various sectors have been instrumental in forging a path where technology enhances independence and societal involvement.

NLP's role in bridging communication gaps for those with physical limitations is two-pronged. It provides a much-needed alternative for individuals who find traditional communication methods challenging, and advanced tools like eye-tracking systems exemplify this innovation. These systems, integrated with NLP, allow for control through eye movements, offering an intuitive way for users to interact with technology. This capability of NLP to interpret and predict user intentions is a cornerstone in developing more accessible communication methods.

The evolution of devices integrating Natural Language Processing from basic aids to empowering instruments marks a significant leap forward. These technologies extend beyond facilitating digital connections; they create new paths for social interaction and professional growth. By enhancing user abilities and fostering independence, they redefine the field of assistive technology, shifting the focus from merely compensating for limitations to amplifying capabilities.

Ongoing advancements in assistive technologies depend greatly on feedback from those they are designed to help. Collaboration with the motor-impaired community is essential to customize these technologies to their specific needs. The goal is to develop systems that are proactive and intuitive, offering empowering support. This user-centered approach ensures that these innovations genuinely enhance the lives of their users.

Text-to-speech and voice recognition technologies, for instance, have made substantial progress in supporting individuals with speech impairments. TTS tools translate text into spoken language, allowing users to express their thoughts without speaking. The evolution of TTS has led to more sophisticated systems with diverse voice options and modulation features, enabling greater customization. Customizable speech synthesis, adjusting tone, pitch, and rhythm, achieves a level of realism that closely matches the user's own speech patterns. Such progress in TTS and voice recognition technologies highlights the value of user input in creating more effective, empowering communication tools, mirroring developments for the motor-impaired.

Voice recognition systems have also advanced to accurately interpret the speech of individuals with speech impairments. These intelligent systems are tailored to learn and adapt to a variety of speech irregularities, enabling effective interaction with technology. These improvements have brought a new level of autonomy, easing interactions with smart devices, home automation, and communication apps.

The incorporation of these technologies into mobile devices and computers has opened a world of possibilities for speech-impaired individuals. They can now engage in conversations, control their surroundings, and access services with ease. Offering a degree of independence previously challenging to attain, these technologies allow users to perform everyday tasks such as making phone calls or using virtual assistants, enhancing their autonomy and integration into various aspects of life.

Moreover, the advancement in AI-driven NLP has led to the development of applications that can predict the user's intended words and phrases, enhancing the efficiency of communication. This predictive text technology not only speeds up the communication process but also reduces the cognitive load on the user, making it less strenuous to convey complex thoughts and ideas.

The future of these technologies is particularly promising, with ongoing research focused on making them more adaptive, resilient, and responsive to the nuanced needs of their users. As these tools become more integrated into everyday devices, the barrier between those with speech impairments and the world around them continues to diminish, fostering a more inclusive and accessible environment for all. With continued innovation and dedication, these NLP applications have the potential to completely revolutionize communication for individuals with speech impairments, empowering them to connect and express themselves with confidence and ease.

Deaf and hard-of-hearing individuals are also seeing technologies that are revolutionizing communication, allowing for an environment where sound is no longer a barrier to understanding and interaction. This chapter highlights how NLP serves as a pioneering and transformative tool, facilitating a more inclusive and connected world.

Innovations in sign language recognition represent a significant breakthrough in NLP's application. This technology employs sophisticated algorithms to interpret sign language in real time, effectively bridging the gap between sign language users and those unfamiliar with it. This leap is not just a technical achievement; it's a step towards fostering greater inclusivity and understanding between different languages and cultures. By translating the nuanced gestures of sign language into spoken words or text, this technology erases barriers, enabling fluid communication and connection.

Real-time captioning is another area where NLP shines, converting spoken language into text almost instantaneously. This innovation is crucial in various settings, from classrooms to boardrooms and live broadcasts. It ensures that individuals who are deaf or hard of hearing are not excluded from critical conversations and information streams. The remarkable accuracy and speed of these systems are a testament to the continuous advancement and dedication in the field of NLP.

Beyond these, NLP technologies are advancing to provide auditory experiences through visual or tactile means. Devices that use vibrational feedback and visual alert systems, integrated with NLP, create scenarios where sound is transformed into other sensory forms. This adaptation is particularly vital in situations where audible alerts might be missed, but a visual or tactile signal can provide an essential and timely warning.

A key aspect of these technologies is the focus on user-friendly interfaces, ensuring accessibility for all, regardless of technical proficiency. The goal is to empower users, giving them control and independence through technology, rather than creating a dependency. This approach exemplifies the dedication of NLP researchers and developers to not only innovate but also integrate these technologies seamlessly into the daily lives of the intended users.

These advancements in NLP for the deaf and hard of hearing represent more than just technological achievements; they symbolize a profound commitment to cultivating an empathetic and barrier-free society. As these technologies evolve and synergize with other assistive tools, the possibility for effortless communication expands. We are moving towards a future where communication barriers are not merely reduced but entirely dismantled, courtesy of continuous innovation in NLP. This dedication to inclusivity and understanding is fueling our journey towards a world where everyone's voice is heard and valued. It's a strategic and passionate pursuit, ensuring that no one is left unheard.

Similarly, NLP is playing a transformative role for visually impaired individuals, enhancing their autonomy and comprehension of their environment. This next chapter in the evolution of NLP technologies focuses on how these tools are becoming vital in providing visually impaired people with a clearer sense of the world around them. Just as NLP is bridging communication gaps for the deaf and hard of hearing, it is also creating pathways for the visually impaired to engage more fully with their surroundings. These technologies are not just tools for assistance; they are gateways to a deeper understanding and interaction with the world, empowering individuals with different abilities to experience life more richly and independently.

Audio-based navigation systems are a prime example of NLP's impact. These systems, fueled by sophisticated algorithms, offer more than just directions; they provide verbal descriptions of the user's surroundings, informing about potential obstacles, terrain changes, and the proximity of destinations. This detailed guidance facilitates not only orientation but also ensures safety and confidence for visually impaired users as they navigate through various environments.

Another transformative development in NLP is image recognition technology. These systems interpret visual scenes, converting them into spoken words. They possess the ability to recognize faces, decipher expressions, and read text from various sources like signs or documents. This conversion of visual cues into auditory information is not just a technological achievement but a significant leap in making everyday visual information accessible to those without sight.

Voice-assisted interfaces represent another remarkable stride in this field. These interfaces allow users to interact with technology through natural speech, understanding everyday language, and responding in kind. Visually impaired users can thus perform a wide array of tasks, from simple functions like setting alarms to more complex operations like retrieving information from the internet, all through intuitive voice commands.

The integration of NLP in these technologies isn't just about creating standalone tools; it's about developing an ecosystem that supports visually impaired individuals in various life aspects. This includes academic tools that articulate graphical data in textbooks and systems that translate visual content in real-time during events. The scope of these technologies is vast and continuously evolving.

Looking ahead, the horizon of NLP technology holds even more sophisticated aids for the visually impaired. Expectations are set on enhanced scene descriptions, deeper contextual understanding, and predictive assistance tailored to individual preferences and behaviors. These forthcoming advancements stem not just from technological progress but also from the concerted efforts of developers, accessibility advocates, and the visually impaired community. Their collective endeavor is geared towards achieving a universal design that's fully inclusive, aiming to ensure that individuals with visual impairments can navigate the world as effortlessly as their sighted peers. This commitment to pushing the boundaries of NLP for inclusivity is not merely empowering; it's a transformative force, charting a future where visual impairment does not restrict access to the diversity and richness of the world.

The transformative impact of Natural Language Processing extends beyond assisting the visually impaired and is also revolutionizing education, particularly for students with disabilities. Its significant role in education is manifested in its ability to customize learning experiences, making educational resources adaptive and accessible. For students grappling with reading difficulties or cognitive impairments, the technology's ability to convert text to speech or simplify complex materials proves invaluable.

These advancements nurture an inclusive educational setting where every student, regardless of their learning needs, can access and engage with content in a way that suits them best.

A critical question emerges: How is this technology enhancing educational experiences for students with disabilities? By tailoring educational content to various learning styles and abilities, it enables more effective learning. For example, it can transform complex texts into simpler language, aiding comprehension for students with cognitive challenges. Such adaptability is key to fostering an inclusive classroom where all students have equal access to educational resources.

This technology also shines in assessment and feedback, with intelligent systems capable of precisely analyzing student responses and delivering immediate, personalized feedback. This aspect is especially beneficial for students with disabilities, ensuring they receive the same level of feedback and support as their peers and promoting fairness in education. The real-time capabilities of these assessment tools also allow educators to monitor student progress and tailor teaching strategies to individual learning needs, ensuring every student has the chance to excel.

Developing and refining these tools necessitates collaboration among developers, educators, and members of the differently-abled community. This collaboration is essential to pinpoint gaps in current educational technologies and steer the development of applications that effectively cater to the varied learning needs of all students.

Expanding on this transformative power, NLP-enabled tools are reshaping education by allowing for the customization of content to match the unique learning profiles of differently-abled students. This customization aids in understanding and retention, and respects the individual learning journeys of students. Educational content, once limited in its format, can now be dynamically altered to suit various learning styles, such as converting text to speech for auditory learners or offering interactive experiences for those who benefit from engagement beyond traditional reading.

The impact of NLP on assessment and feedback mechanisms is equally significant. It enables educators to provide real-time, personalized support and adapt their teaching strategies to maximize each student's learning potential. For example, NLP tools can analyze a student's work for grammar and style while assessing comprehension through adaptive quizzes.

Collaboration between NLP developers, educational experts, and the differently-abled community plays a pivotal role in the creation of effective and inclusive learning tools. This partnership ensures that the developed technologies are not only advanced in their technical capabilities but also pedagogically sound and responsive to the diverse needs of learners. By integrating the insights of educators and the lived experiences of differently-abled individuals, these tools are finely tuned for maximum effectiveness and inclusivity. Furthermore, NLP technologies provide essential support in resource-limited classrooms, enabling personalized attention that might otherwise be challenging to deliver. They serve as a vital aid for educators, facilitating equitable access to customized learning experiences.

This ethos of collaboration and tailored design naturally leads into the specific approach required in developing NLP applications for differently-abled individuals. In this realm, user-centered design becomes paramount. By adopting this methodology, developers focus on crafting technologies that are expressly designed to meet the unique needs of these users from the very beginning. Prioritizing end-users in the design process allows for the creation of interfaces that are not just accessible, but truly resonate with the individuals they are intended to assist. Such a focused approach results in intuitive, efficient, and empowering tools, specifically crafted to enhance the capabilities and independence of individuals with disabilities.

A crucial question arises: How does user-centered design ensure that NLP applications are truly accessible and empowering for differently-abled individuals? The answer lies in the design process itself, which emphasizes understanding and addressing the specific needs of these users. By involving the target demographic in accessibility testing, developers can identify and rectify usability issues that may not be apparent to those without disabilities. This hands-on, proactive approach is key to refining the user experience, ensuring that the tools serve as a bridge to greater independence.

Another critical aspect is addressing bias and ensuring fairness in NLP algorithms. Algorithms can inadvertently inherit biases from their training data, leading to outcomes that may perpetuate social inequalities. Incorporating fairness into algorithmic design is crucial for mitigating these biases, thus promoting equity and preventing discriminatory practices.

Engaging with differently-abled communities in the development process is both ethical and strategic. Such engagement fosters empathy and a deeper understanding of the challenges these individuals face. This understanding is essential for effective design, ensuring that the developed tools truly reflect the needs and preferences of the users.

Inclusive design in NLP applications transcends mere compliance with standards or reactive feedback. It embodies a visionary, empathetic, and strategic approach that anticipates needs and innovates to meet them. This philosophy aims to create a transformative, resilient, and sustainable technological ecosystem that acknowledges the universal benefits of accessibility. This user-first philosophy is a benchmark for excellence in NLP and is crucial for building a truly inclusive digital world.

The commitment to user-centered design in NLP applications involves a profound understanding of end-users, especially those with different abilities. Collaborating closely with differently-abled communities, designers and developers gain insights that guide the creation of intuitive and adaptive technologies. This collaborative approach ensures that solutions genuinely enhance the quality of life for these users.

Inclusivity in design requires rigorous accessibility testing, where applications are iteratively evaluated with real users to ensure comfort and usability for everyone. These evaluations might reveal needs for adjustable text sizes, alternative input methods, or simplified workflows, which are essential for the practical use of technology in daily life.

Confronting bias in NLP systems is another pillar of ethical AI development. Developers must employ strategies like diversifying data and implementing fairness metrics to prevent discriminatory outcomes. Continuous monitoring for bias is crucial, allowing for the ongoing adjustment of NLP systems to align with societal values.

Engagement with differently-abled users in NLP tool development cultivates a culture of understanding and respect. This vital interaction ensures that NLP technologies affirm dignity and promote independence, transcending mere task performance. Moreover, such engagement raises societal awareness, spotlighting the unique challenges faced by differently-abled individuals and encouraging a broader conversation on accessibility and inclusivity.

This increased awareness segues into the complexities faced in the development of NLP technologies, particularly when it comes to breaking down language and cultural barriers. In the pursuit of truly inclusive NLP tools, developers must navigate a path rich with linguistic and cultural diversity. An agile, culturally sensitive approach is essential, one that not only recognizes but embraces linguistic differences. Successful development hinges on a collaborative synergy involving developers, researchers, and user communities. Each group plays a pivotal role: developers bring their technical expertise, researchers offer insights into the nuances of language processing, and communities provide a thorough understanding of cultural contexts. This multidisciplinary collaboration is key to creating NLP applications that are not only functional but also culturally sensitive and relevant.

A key challenge in this field is developing language models that can interpret a multitude of languages and dialects. These models must be robust and adaptable, capable of understanding the intricacies of human language, including idiomatic expressions, regional slang, and non-standard syntax. This complexity is essential for truly inclusive NLP tools.

Furthermore, NLP tools must be designed with a global perspective, considering the wide variety of cultural norms and communication styles. This demands a visionary methodology, ensuring tools are developed and fine-tuned with an authentic understanding of users' cultural backgrounds. Such a global approach to NLP also requires proactive measures to address and overcome inherent biases within the technology. By integrating diverse datasets and including underrepresented languages, NLP can move towards a more equitable representation of linguistic diversity, enhancing the utility of NLP applications and ensuring they serve as empowering tools.

The potential of NLP to revolutionize accessibility for differently-abled individuals is immense. Through dedicated, empathetic, and innovative efforts, developers and researchers can unlock unprecedented opportunities for inclusion, enhancing the lives of individuals with disabilities and enriching our interconnected world.

Addressing the challenge of language and cultural inclusivity in NLP technologies is more than a technical task; it involves understanding linguistic nuances and cultural contexts. Overcoming language barriers involves creating systems that understand idioms, colloquialisms, and dialects, ensuring every user feels seen and heard. This is complex, given the multitude of global languages and dialects.

Cultural inclusivity in NLP technologies requires sensitivity to various cultural contexts and societal norms. For instance, gesture recognition systems must differentiate between culturally specific gestures, and text-to-speech applications must accommodate different speech patterns and intonations. Achieving this level of inclusivity necessitates collaboration among developers, linguists, cultural experts, and community representatives, ensuring technology is linguistically accurate and culturally attuned.

As we conclude this chapter and look through the transformative world of NLP in assistive technologies, it's clear that we stand at the cusp of a new era in inclusivity and accessibility. The remarkable advancements in NLP have not only bridged communication gaps but have also fostered a more empathetic and barrier-free society. Looking ahead, the continuous refinement and innovation in NLP technologies promise a future where limitations are transcended, and the full potential of every individual is realized. This chapter underscores the strategic and passionate pursuit towards a world where technology does not only assist but empowers, ensuring that every voice is heard, every gesture understood, and every challenge overcome.

Chapter 12

NLP for Creativity and Innovation

Have you ever wondered if the surge of digital technology could unlock the deepest wells of human creativity? Picture this: an algorithm not just processing data but sparking a revolution in the way we conceive ideas. This chapter is your guide through a remarkable journey, where Natural Language Processing emerges as the unsung hero of innovation and creativity. It's a tale where machines don't replace human ingenuity but amplify it, where the line between artificial intelligence and artistic inspiration blurs. Join us as we explore how language processing is not just changing but revolutionizing creativity, from the way writers craft stories to how musicians compose melodies. This journey promises to reach an exhilarating climax, revealing the untapped potential of NLP in reshaping the creative processes across various domains.

Being creative has never been easier than in todays technology driven world. This is especially evident when looking at the ways natural language processing has advanced the ideation processes used today. Its ability to sift through and analyze extensive datasets is unmatched. These algorithms can unveil trends and correlations that escape human notice, providing a fertile ground for groundbreaking ideas.

Imagine an NLP-powered brainstorming tool that not only recommends ideas but also connects them to emerging trends, relevant data points, and even parallel innovations in different industries. Such tools can significantly expedite the brainstorming process, pushing teams towards more original and viable solutions.

Moreover, NLP facilitates dynamic collaboration. Idea recommendation systems can act as virtual facilitators, prompting discussions with questions or scenarios crafted from the analysis of vast amounts of text-based data. This can result in a more structured and fruitful brainstorming session, especially in diverse teams where varying expertise can be bridged effectively.

NLP's impact on idea generation is not just about the quantity of ideas produced but also their quality. By providing a diverse array of starting points and perspectives, NLP ensures that the ideation process is not confined to the familiar boundaries of human experience. Instead, it becomes an expansive, data-driven exploration of possibilities.

In addition, these technologies can aid in overcoming the cognitive biases that often limit human ideation. By presenting data-driven insights and objectively generated ideas, NLP tools can help teams break away from their preconceived notions and explore uncharted territories.

The potential of Natural Language Processing in ideation and creativity is vast. As this technology advances, its role in creative processes is set to not just streamline but also enrich brainstorming. By blending its computational abilities with an intricate understanding of human creativity, we are approaching a new chapter in idea generation — one characterized by inclusivity, diversity, and innovation.

Its application in creative writing signifies a transformative phase in the literary world. Sentiment analysis, a notable capability of this technology, offers writers a deep insight into the emotional depth of their work. This feature can evaluate text to pinpoint and classify emotions like joy, sadness, anger, or excitement. Writers can use this analysis to fine-tune their narratives, ensuring the emotional undercurrents are in line with their intended effect on readers.

Language generation algorithms are at the forefront of content creation, presenting a fountain of ideas and suggestions to spark an author's imagination. These advanced systems can propose plot twists, character traits, or dialogues, acting as a novel source of inspiration. The aim here is not to supplant the author's distinct voice, but to enhance their creative process with a range of options, weaving a narrative that embodies both authenticity and originality.

Writing assistants powered by this technology have become crucial for authors, refining their manuscripts meticulously. These tools excel in improving grammar, syntax, and readability. By simplifying the editing process, authors can devote more attention to the creative facets of their work, rather than the intricacies of language. The outcome is a manuscript that is not only grammatically accurate but also fluid and lucid, allowing the writer's ideas to be conveyed clearly and effectively.

Moreover, these technologies are pioneering in their ability to adapt to the writer's style, creating a personalized experience. Such customization ensures that the writer's voice remains distinct and undiluted while benefiting from the precision and efficiency of NLP. As these tools continue to evolve, they will become even more intuitive, learning from each interaction with the author to provide increasingly tailored assistance.

The future of NLP in creative writing is boundless, promising a synergy between human creativity and artificial intelligence. As these tools become more integrated into the writing process, they promise to empower authors with an expanded toolkit for storytelling, transforming how stories are crafted and experienced. This intersection of technology and creativity holds the potential not just to streamline the writing process but to revolutionize the very essence of story construction, inviting writers to push the boundaries of their work.

The intersection of NLP and visual arts forges a dynamic space where the boundary between technology and human creativity blurs. Image recognition algorithms, when interlaced with NLP, can dissect and interpret visual data, offering insights that were once solely within the purview of human perception. These systems can identify patterns, themes, and emotions within visual content, providing artists and designers with a rich tapestry of information to inform their creations.

This fusion of visual analysis and linguistic interpretation opens up new avenues for artistic collaboration. For instance, a designer can present a mood board to an NLP-enhanced system, which can then analyze the imagery, extract thematic elements, and suggest verbal concepts that align with the visual stimuli. These suggestions can inspire conceptual and non-conceptual frameworks that the artist may not have initially considered, potentially leading to groundbreaking work.

In design processes, the application of NLP can streamline and enrich the brainstorming phase. Designers often seek to convey complex messages through visual media; NLP tools can assist by suggesting motifs or design elements that align with the intended message. Moreover, they can provide alternative viewpoints or cultural nuances, ensuring that the designs resonate with a wider audience and maintain cultural sensitivity.

The creative suggestions offered by these advanced algorithms are not prescriptive but rather serve as a springboard for the artist's own imagination. They act as a catalyst, triggering new connections and ideas that may have lain dormant. This partnership between human and machine does not diminish the artist's role but rather amplifies their creative potential, allowing them to explore uncharted artistic ideas with confidence.

Looking forward, the potential for NLP to transform visual arts and design is vast. As algorithms become more sophisticated and attuned to the nuances of human creativity, they will provide even more nuanced and contextually rich suggestions. The canvas of possibility is large, and NLP stands to be a valuable ally in the quest for innovative and meaningful artistic expression. This synergy between artist and technology is a testament to the era we are entering—an era where art and Artificial Intelligence collaborate to create works that are both technologically advanced and deeply human.

Looking at the music industry, NLP's entry marks a significant stride towards a more nuanced and personalized listening experience. Through the analysis of lyrics and musical structures, NLP algorithms are adept at discerning mood, theme, and even the emotional trajectory of songs. This analytical capacity allows for the curation of playlists that are not just genre-specific but attuned to the listener's current emotional state or desired ambiance.

For musicians and composers, NLP serves as a digital muse. Composition tools equipped with NLP can offer melodic suggestions based on a vast database of musical compositions, providing a variety of harmonic structures and chord progressions that resonate with the artist's initial concept. This not only accelerates the creative process but also introduces artists to a broader spectrum of musical possibilities, influencing the emergence of new genres and sounds.

Furthermore, NLP-driven music software can analyze an artist's previous works to identify signature elements, then suggest new ways to evolve their musical style while retaining their unique sound. By drawing on the vast expanse of music history, these tools provide historical context, enabling artists to create music that pays homage to traditional styles while pushing the envelope of innovation.

Language processing tools can personalize learning music education, by adapting to a student's progress, suggesting exercises to improve weak areas, or introducing new concepts when ready. This tailors the educational experience to individual needs, allowing for a more effective and enjoyable learning process.

The potential of NLP in music extends to live performances, where real-time feedback on audience reactions could shape setlists or the direction of a performance. By analyzing social media feeds and audience engagement, NLP systems could help artists understand which songs resonate most and tailor their performances accordingly.

Looking ahead, the fusion of Natural Language Processing and music is poised to enrich the creative domain. The combination of algorithmic precision with human creativity may become a groundbreaking development in music creation and enjoyment, leading to a more interactive and customized auditory experience.

In the realms of advertising and marketing, the integration of this technology has revolutionized how consumer engagement is approached. Using sentiment analysis, marketers can delve into vast data from social media, reviews, and feedback to understand the public's true reaction to products, campaigns, and brand perception. This knowledge enables a dynamic and responsive marketing approach, where messages are tailored in real-time to align with the audience's emotions.

Language generation algorithms further enhance the creative process, providing marketers with tools to craft compelling narratives that embody their brand's essence. These algorithms can create diverse and innovative ad content, which marketers can then refine to meet their strategic goals. The outcome is a message that is not only engaging but also relevant, distinguishing it in a competitive market.

Moreover, this technology allows for a deeper grasp of consumer language and semantics, enabling brands to communicate in their audience's language. This not only makes the brand more relatable but also improves the effectiveness of keyword targeting in SEO and SEM campaigns, ensuring that marketing efforts reach the most receptive audience.

Additionally, predictive analytics through this technology can anticipate market trends and consumer behaviors, allowing companies to act proactively. Understanding consumer interests and sentiments in advance, marketers can design campaigns that address emerging needs before they become evident to the consumer.

Chatbots and virtual assistants, powered by this technology, offer personalized customer experiences, engaging consumers in valuable conversations and guiding them through the purchasing process. These data-rich interactions contribute to the marketing ecosystem, creating a continuous feedback loop that refines and personalizes the user experience.

In the dynamic world of digital marketing, this technology is a foundational tool that not only streamlines operations but also boosts creative potential. As brands aim to create meaningful connections with their audience, this technology becomes an essential partner, transforming data into insights, insights into strategies, and strategies into compelling narratives that deeply resonate with audiences.

Utilizing this technology in product development sparks innovation by converting customer conversations and market data into actionable insights. By dissecting customer feedback and sentiments across various platforms, algorithms can identify subtle preferences and emerging trends that might be overlooked by conventional analysis. This insight is vital for product innovation, uncovering market gaps and opportunities for differentiation.

Beyond identifying trends, this technology supports dynamic ideation processes. It assists teams in understanding complex customer needs, market conditions, and possible technological innovations. For example, by aggregating and analyzing customer service transcripts, product reviews, and forum discussions, it can offer a comprehensive view of customer challenges and desires.

NLP-powered ideation platforms act as catalysts for collaborative creativity, breaking down silos between departments. They foster an environment where insights from sales, customer service, and R&D converge, enabling multidisciplinary teams to brainstorm and innovate with a holistic view of the consumer experience. These platforms can also suggest concepts and improvements by identifying patterns and associations within data that human analysis might miss.

In the iterative cycle of product development, NLP accelerates the prototyping phase by enabling rapid feedback loops. Real-time analysis of consumer reactions to a product concept can guide immediate refinements, shortening the time from ideation to market launch. This agility is critical in today's fast-paced market where consumer preferences are continually evolving.

Moreover, NLP enhances the personalization of products. By understanding individual customer language and behavior patterns, companies can tailor their products to meet the specific needs of different market segments or even individual consumers.

As the nexus between data intelligence and human creativity, NLP empowers companies to not just keep pace with market evolution but to lead it. Through its ability to distill vast amounts of unstructured data into clear signals, NLP equips product developers with a compass to navigate toward true innovation, ensuring that new products resonate deeply with consumer needs and aspirations. This strategic application of NLP not only fortifies a company's competitive edge but also amplifies its capacity to deliver groundbreaking products that define the future of the market.

Looking at how natural language processing and data visualization work together, we find a dynamic space where data is not just seen but experienced. Here, algorithms can dissect vast datasets, identifying and elevating crucial insights into visual formats that narrate the story behind the numbers. This transformation from data points to visual stories is not just a technical process; it's an art form.

Imagine a dashboard that not only displays figures but also highlights patterns and trends through interactive charts and graphs, which adapt in real-time as new data flows in. This adaptability is a testament to the power of NLP in creating responsive visualizations that evolve with the underlying data.

Moreover, when it comes to storytelling, NLP tools stand as ingenious narrators. They can distill complex ideas from texts to picking out the central themes, and weave them into interactive experiences. These tools can generate summaries, identify sentiment trends, and even suggest objective structures that best fit the extracted themes.

Such storytelling is not just about relaying facts but instead engaging audiences on a deeper level. By creating stories that respond to user interaction, these tools invite the audience to become part of the story. This level of engagement ensures that the message is not just delivered but felt and understood.

For communicators and educators, this means that their messages can be made resonant to a wider audience, transcending the barriers of technical jargon. By using NLP to create visual and text aids, they can ensure their insights don't just inform but also inspire.

As these technologies continue to advance, the future of data communication is poised to become more intuitive, immersive, and ultimately, more human. The blend of NLP with data visualization and storytelling is not merely a technological advancement; it's a leap towards making information not just accessible but also emotionally resonant.

NLP's interdisciplinary nature serves as a conduit for cross-domain synthesis, where insights from distinct industries can spark innovation in another. For instance, an NLP system analyzing data within the healthcare sector can uncover patterns in patient care, which, when applied to customer service in the hospitality industry, could revolutionize the customer experience. This transference of knowledge and strategies across sectors is what makes NLP a potent tool for innovation.

The algorithms can ingest a multitude of data types – from academic research papers to social media trends, and from customer feedback in retail to best practices in manufacturing. By doing so, they can detect latent correlations and draw parallels that may suggest novel approaches in seemingly unrelated fields. For example, a linguistic pattern observed in successful marketing campaigns might inspire the development of persuasive communication strategies for public health messaging.

Furthermore, NLP facilitates the distillation of complex information into accessible knowledge, making it easier for professionals to step outside their domains and explore new concepts. This ability to 'translate' specialized language into a more generalized understanding promotes interdisciplinary collaboration. It could enable a financial analyst to draw on breakthroughs in machine learning from the tech industry to enhance predictive models in finance.

In creative realms, NLP can offer artists and designers unconventional inspiration by analyzing and interpreting data from science and technology, suggesting ways to incorporate advanced materials or sustainable practices into their work. Conversely, an engineering problem might find a solution in the aesthetics of art or the ergonomics of design, identified through NLP's data-driven insights.

NLP-powered tools also democratize access to cross-domain knowledge, which was once siloed within expert communities. By providing laypersons with the essence of complex subjects, these tools empower a wider audience to participate in innovation processes. For example, an entrepreneur with access to NLP-extracted insights from cutting-edge biotechnology research could ideate a startup that brings advanced science to the consumer market.

The impact of such cross-domain fertilization is profound. It not only stimulates the generation of innovative products and services but also propels societal progress. By uncovering interconnectedness between varied disciplines, NLP acts as a catalyst for comprehensive solutions to multifaceted problems, driving forward human ingenuity and the development of a more interconnected and progressive society.

NLP technologies have become invaluable allies in surmounting creative blocks, providing an array of tools to catalyze the creative process. One such tool is the idea generation platform that uses NLP to offer thought-provoking prompts and brainstorming assistance. These platforms can analyze previous works or trends to suggest new angles and ideas, propelling creators past moments of stagnation.

For writers, NLP applications can suggest story developments, character traits, or plot twists based on the analysis of literary databases, helping authors to weave more intricate and engaging stories. For visual arts, natural language processing can analyze a painter's color usage and style to propose new combinations or techniques that might resonate with the artist's evolving aesthetic.

Beyond generating ideas, NLP is instrumental in mood and sentiment analysis, which can be leveraged to craft a supportive creative atmosphere. By interpreting emotional cues in written journals or social media posts, NLP tools can help individuals recognize patterns in their mood and suggest activities or changes in routine to foster a more productive mindset.

Furthermore, NLP-driven analytics can identify the linguistic markers associated with creative flow in personal writing or during brainstorming sessions, giving individuals insights into their own creative rhythms and optimal conditions for innovation. This can lead to personalized strategies for enhancing creativity, such as adjusting the environment, experimenting with different times for creative work, or even varying the medium of expression.

In collaborative settings, NLP tools can analyze group communication to facilitate more effective brainstorming sessions. By identifying the most fruitful discussions and pinpointing moments when the creative energy peaks, these tools can guide teams in harnessing their collective creativity more efficiently.

These applications of NLP not only provide immediate assistance in overcoming creative hurdles but also contribute to a deeper understanding of the creative process itself. As creators become more attuned to the patterns and conditions that drive their creativity, they can strategically deploy NLP tools to sustain a more consistently productive and innovative workflow, turning what was once a sporadic burst of inspiration into a well-honed craft.

Wrapping out this chapter, its important to look at the ethical considerations of NLP, and how various software that use NLP can affect entire industries for the better or worse. This was just seen with the Hollywood strikes of 2023, where various unions were striking against AI.

As the fusion of NLP with creative endeavors becomes increasingly common, the imperative for ethical vigilance grows. NLP systems, while advancing creativity, must be carefully calibrated to avoid embedding or amplifying biases. Algorithmic bias can skew the diversity of generated content, leading to homogeneity that stifles true creativity. Developers must thus prioritize the creation of unbiased algorithms and the curating of diverse training data.

Privacy emerges as another pivotal concern. NLP tools often require access to personal data for customized suggestions. Safeguarding this data against unauthorized access is paramount to maintaining trust. The use of such personal data must be transparent, and consent must be obtained, ensuring that users retain control over their information.

Intellectual property rights stand at the forefront of ethical considerations in NLP-enabled creativity. The lines between inspiration and infringement blur when algorithms generate content based on existing works. Clear guidelines and policies must be established to determine ownership and proper attribution of algorithmically generated content, ensuring creators receive due recognition and compensation for their original work.

Furthermore, the deployment of NLP must consider the impact on the creative industry. The democratization of creativity through NLP tools should not devalue the skills and contributions of human artists. Instead, NLP should be positioned as a collaborative tool that enhances human creativity rather than replaces it.

Ethical frameworks and guidelines are essential for the responsible integration of NLP in the creative process. Regular audits and updates of NLP systems help maintain ethical standards, while collaboration with ethicists, legal experts, and the creative community ensures that NLP tools are used in a manner that respects and uplifts the human element of creativity.

By addressing these ethical challenges head-on, the integration of NLP into creativity can progress in a manner that not only fosters innovation but also aligns with societal values and the collective good. This conscientious approach will ensure that the creative potential of NLP is realized in a way that is fair, respectful, and beneficial for all involved.

As we conclude this fascinating exploration into the world of NLP and creativity, we find ourselves at a pivotal point where technology and human ingenuity converge. This chapter has taken us on an extraordinary journey, unveiling the transformative impact of NLP across diverse creative domains. We've witnessed how NLP, once a tool primarily for data analysis, has become a dynamic force in fostering innovation and creativity.

We have seen NLP redefine the boundaries of artistic expression, enabling writers, artists, and musicians to explore new realms of creativity. From generating unique story plots to suggesting harmonious melodies, NLP has proven to be an invaluable partner in the creative process. Its role in sentiment analysis has provided a deeper understanding of emotional resonance, allowing creators to fine-tune their work to achieve the desired impact.

Moreover, the integration of NLP in visual arts and design has opened up new avenues for artistic collaboration, blending the precision of algorithms with the fluidity of human creativity. In the music industry, NLP has ushered in a new era of personalized listening experiences, tailoring content to the listener's mood and preferences.

Yet, as we embrace these advancements, we must also navigate the ethical implications that accompany this integration of technology and creativity. Addressing issues of privacy, bias, and intellectual property rights are not just challenges but responsibilities that come with the territory of innovation. Ensuring that NLP enhances rather than replaces human creativity is crucial in maintaining the integrity and value of artistic work.

In closing, the journey through NLP's role in creativity leaves us with a profound realization. The future of creativity is not a solitary path but a collaborative journey where technology serves as a catalyst, unlocking new possibilities and empowering creators to reach new heights. As we look ahead, it's clear that NLP will continue to be a key player in this exciting and ever-evolving world of creativity and innovation.

Chapter 13

The Transformative Power of NLP

Can you imagine a world where every interaction with technology is as natural and intuitive as a conversation with a close friend? Picture a world where machines understand not just your words, but your emotions and intentions. Welcome to the transformative world of Natural Language Processing – a realm where the line between human and machine communication blurs. This chapter unfolds the story of NLP's remarkable journey, from its early steps to becoming a cornerstone of modern digital interactions. We'll look into a case study of a company that harnessed NLP to revolutionize its customer service, a story that will reveal the profound impact of this technology. Prepare to be enthralled by the power of NLP in bridging the gap between digital sophistication and human empathy.

Redefining interactions and expectations in customer service is being redefined by NLP. Virtual assistants and chatbots, as discussed in prior chapters, empowered by NLP, have shifted the paradigm from one-size-fits-all to tailor-made customer experiences. These AI-driven systems can understand and process natural human language, enabling them to respond to customer inquiries with precision and a semblance of empathy.

By interpreting the tone and emotion behind customer queries, businesses can fine-tune their support strategies. This technology not only deciphers textual communication but also senses the customer's satisfaction level, allowing companies to respond proactively to unspoken concerns.

These NLP systems excel in their tireless availability, providing answers and support around the clock. This 24/7 service capability ensures that customer needs are met promptly, a vital element in maintaining customer trust and building long-term loyalty.

Moreover, NLP tools are continually learning from interactions, growing more adept at handling complex queries and providing accurate, relevant information. This self-improving nature of NLP technologies means that they can keep pace with evolving customer needs and expectations.

Businesses leveraging NLP in customer service not only elevate the user experience but also gain valuable insights into customer preferences and behaviors. These insights can drive strategic decisions, from product development to marketing approaches, anchoring the business more firmly in customer-centric practices.

In operational contexts, the integration of NLP signifies a significant shift towards more intelligent and automated systems. This evolution is characterized by the transition from manual and labor-intensive tasks to solutions that are efficient and scalable. NLP enables the automation of processes such as data entry, scheduling, and customer inquiries, which traditionally consumed considerable human resources.

NLP is particularly transformative in the realm of data analysis. Here, it can sift through vast quantities of unstructured data — from customer feedback to market reports — extracting relevant insights that drive strategic decisions. This capability is not just a facilitator of efficiency; it also enhances the accuracy and speed at which businesses can respond to market dynamics.

Supply chain operations benefit from NLP through improved communication channels. Bots equipped with NLP can interact with suppliers and manage transactions with unprecedented ease, reducing errors and enhancing the flow of information. These advancements contribute to a more resilient supply chain, capable of adapting to unforeseen events or shifts in demand.

Moreover, NLP tools can optimize internal communications within organizations. By summarizing emails, categorizing correspondence, and highlighting action items, these tools help streamline internal workflows, thus freeing employees to focus on more complex, value-adding tasks.

In knowledge management, NLP stands out by structuring and categorizing information, making it readily accessible and useful. This empowers organizations to capitalize on their collective knowledge, fostering a culture of continuous learning and improvement.

For businesses, the adoption of NLP in operations leads to a more agile and responsive infrastructure, prepared to meet the challenges of today's fast-paced market environment. It is not simply about replacing human effort but augmenting and enhancing it with intelligent automation that can learn, adapt, and provide insights that were previously unattainable. The future of operational efficiency is here, and it speaks the language of NLP.

Today, data breaches and cyber threats loom large. NPL's deployment in the world of cybersecurity and fraud detection is not just innovative, but essential. By dissecting the language and patterns within communication data, NLP algorithms can discern inconsistencies and irregularities that may indicate deceitful behavior or emerging security threats.

These algorithms trawl through emails, transaction records, and online interactions, flagging potential frauds that escape the human eye. For instance, in financial transactions, NLP can analyze the linguistic nuances of client communication to detect phishing attempts or fraudulent requests. It can assess risk by evaluating the sentiment and authenticity of messages, providing an additional layer of security.

In cybersecurity, NLP contributes to the fortification of digital fortresses by identifying and interpreting the chatter that may signal a brewing cyber-attack. It can monitor and analyze data from various sources, such as social media, forums, and dark web marketplaces, where cyber threats often gestate. By processing this information, NLP can alert human analysts to potential vulnerabilities and breaches, enabling preemptive action.

Furthermore, Natural Language Processing aids in automating threat reports and amalgamating data from various cybersecurity tools, offering comprehensive insights into potential security risks. This integration of information helps businesses construct a detailed understanding of their security environment, ensuring that protective measures are both precise and efficient.

This technology's role in detecting threats and ensuring regulatory compliance is critical, especially in monitoring communications for adherence to legal standards, thereby mitigating risks. Its ability to comprehend and interpret human language positions it as an indispensable asset in countering digital wrongdoing. As it progresses, it not only keeps up with malevolent actors but often outpaces them, playing a pivotal role in upholding the trust foundational to the digital economy. Its ongoing development is key to safeguarding the security and integrity of our digital interactions.

The same capacity for advanced data processing makes this technology invaluable in managing the current deluge of information. Functioning as sophisticated filters, these technologies adeptly extract meaningful insights from the ever-expanding ocean of data. Acting like digital sieves, they identify and distill the most pertinent information, allowing users to focus on crucial insights amid the vast volume of digital content. This capability in data management and interpretation is not just a demonstration of the technology's strength but is also essential in aiding users to make informed decisions in an information-rich world.

These tools appear in various forms. Summarization algorithms, for example, condense extensive documents into brief summaries, retaining key information while omitting superfluous details. This feature revolutionizes how professionals handle literature reviews, market analyses, and research, saving significant time and boosting efficiency.

Filtering systems, another application of this technology, sort through emails, news feeds, and notifications, prioritizing content based on user preferences and historical behavior. These systems evolve over time, increasingly aligning with the user's interests and requirements, ensuring that their digital space is both pertinent and manageable.

Organizational tools go a step further, clustering related information and categorizing data into intuitive hierarchies. This not only aids in information retrieval but also in knowledge discovery, as it illuminates connections between seemingly disparate pieces of data.

In business contexts, these NLP applications synthesize market reports, customer feedback, and competitive intelligence into actionable insights. For individuals, they streamline the continuous flow of news, communications, and social media into curated streams that enhance learning and personal growth.

The potential of NLP to cut through information clutter is crucial as the volume and velocity of data generation accelerate. It offers a compass in the informational wilderness, guiding users to clarity and insight. As these technologies evolve, they will become ever more adept at elevating the signal above the noise, enabling both individuals and organizations to make more enlightened decisions in an increasingly complex world.

Personal virtual assistants have become indispensable companions in the modern world, simplifying the complexities of day-to-day life. With the integration of NLP, these assistants go beyond mere voice commands, understanding the context and nuances of human language, making interactions more fluid and intuitive. They act as personal managers, deftly handling schedules and reminders. For instance, they can schedule meetings, considering all participants' availability and time zones, and even suggest optimal meeting lengths based on past preferences.

These intelligent systems can also curate information and entertainment based on the user's history and preferences, from news briefings to music selection. By analyzing previous interactions and choices, they provide recommendations that feel uniquely tailored, making discovery an effortless part of daily life.

Moreover, personal virtual assistants have evolved to act as proactive aides. They remind users of upcoming bills, track package deliveries, and can even suggest the best time to leave for an appointment by monitoring traffic patterns — all without prompt. Their ability to integrate with smart home devices allows for a seamless control of the living environment, from adjusting thermostats to securing locks, all through simple voice commands.

In professional settings, these assistants are revolutionizing efficiency. They transcribe meeting notes, manage emails, and even assist in drafting responses by understanding the intent and content of the conversation. This level of assistance is redefining productivity, allowing professionals to allocate their time to more critical, creative tasks.

As these NLP-driven assistants evolve, they continue to adapt to individual speech patterns, regional dialects, and languages, making them more inclusive and accessible to a wider audience. They're not just tools but collaborative partners that learn and grow with their users.

The future of personal virtual assistants is one where the line between user and technology blurs, creating a partnership that intuitively anticipates needs and preferences. The meticulous orchestration of daily tasks by these assistants represents a leap forward in personal time management and productivity, making everyday life not just manageable but more enjoyable. The key to these advancements is the thoughtful implementation of NLP, ensuring that as the technology grows, it does so with the user's best interests at heart.

In the educational sector, NLP personalizes the learning experience in unprecedented ways. Adaptive learning systems, powered by NLP, tailor educational content to match the learning pace and style of each individual. These intelligent systems analyze learner responses, predict areas of difficulty, and present material in ways that enhance understanding and retention.

Interactive tutoring systems, another application of NLP, simulate one-on-one instruction. They engage learners in natural dialogue, answer questions, provide explanations, and offer feedback that is immediate and constructive. This interaction mimics a personalized tutoring session, making education accessible anytime and anywhere.

Moreover, NLP facilitates the assessment of written assignments with nuanced understanding, evaluating not just the content but also the use of language, the structure of arguments, and the originality of thought. This capability supports educators in providing detailed feedback, enabling a deeper insight into a learner's comprehension and areas for improvement.

Language learning applications with NLP at their core offer an immersive experience. They listen to pronunciation, provide corrections, and guide learners through complex language nuances. By conversing with these applications, language learners practice real-world communication, gaining confidence and proficiency.

NLP's influence extends to special education, where tools customize learning experiences for individuals with unique challenges, ensuring no learner is left behind. These systems adapt to various needs, from language deficiencies to auditory and visual processing issues, allowing for an inclusive educational environment.

As educators harness the power of NLP, they gain insights into learning patterns and outcomes, paving the way for data-driven strategies that can uplift the entire educational framework. This symbiosis of technology and education promises a future where learning is a lifelong, accessible, and fully personalized journey, breaking down barriers to knowledge and skill acquisition.

The integration of NLP into human-machine interfaces marks a significant leap in technological evolution. Voice-activated devices and sophisticated chatbots are now capable of understanding context, emotion, and subtleties in human language, creating a more intuitive and frictionless user experience.

Voice-activated technology, for instance, has transcended simple command-and-response interactions. These systems now detect nuances in speech, such as intonation and stress, to comprehend user intent more accurately. Users can speak to devices as they would a human, with the technology often able to follow complex lines of conversation, manage tasks, and provide information seamlessly.

Natural language process has enabled a shift from rigid, scripted responses to dynamic dialogues with chatbots. These Modern chatbots can conduct conversations that feel natural, learning from past interactions to improve future responses. They are becoming adept at detecting user frustration or confusion, allowing them to adapt their responses or escalate the issue to a human operator when necessary.

The sophistication of these NLP systems also brings a new level of personalization to user interactions. By analyzing speech patterns and previous interactions, systems can tailor their responses to individual user preferences and history, providing a service that feels personal and considerate.

Moreover, the integration of NLP with other technologies, such as augmented reality and virtual reality, has opened up new dimensions of interaction. Users can now control and navigate complex virtual environments using natural language, making these advanced technologies more accessible to a broader audience.

Businesses and developers are also leveraging NLP to create assistive technologies that offer support for individuals with disabilities, making technology more inclusive. From aiding those with visual impairments through descriptive audio guides to helping those with speech impairments communicate more effectively, NLP is breaking down barriers and opening up the digital world to all.

As NLP technologies continue to mature, the potential for human-like interactions with machines grows. This progress promises a future where technology understands not just the words we say but also the meaning and emotions behind them, leading to a world where machines can assist humans in more meaningful and profound ways.

NLP's integration into accessibility tools marks a transformative era for inclusivity. This technology acts as a bridge for differently-abled individuals, granting them greater autonomy in their interactions with the digital world. Through NLP, devices can be controlled by voice commands, enabling those with motor impairments to navigate interfaces without the need for physical touch. Text-to-speech and speech-to-text functionalities offer those with visual impairments or dyslexia the ability to engage with written content through auditory means.

Furthermore, personalized communication aids designed with NLP allow individuals with speech and language challenges to express themselves clearly. These tools can predict words and form sentences, facilitating smoother conversations. For instance, NLP can empower those with aphasia, improving their ability to communicate by suggesting words and enabling easier construction of sentences.

NLP also enhances the web browsing experience for users with cognitive impairments by simplifying complex language on websites, making information more digestible. By customizing the delivery of content according to the user's specific needs, NLP ensures that everyone has equal access to knowledge and services.

In educational settings, NLP-driven tools support diverse learning needs by adapting materials to suit individual learning styles. These adaptive learning environments can adjust the complexity of text, provide summaries of lengthy documents, and offer quizzes that adapt in difficulty based on the learner's performance.

The impact of NLP in accessibility extends to everyday tasks as well, such as organizing schedules and managing tasks. For individuals who struggle with memory or organizational skills, NLP applications can provide reminders, suggest step-by-step task breakdowns, and even predict potential obstacles, offering solutions in advance.

NLP's role in fostering inclusivity resonates beyond functional assistance; it's about ensuring dignity and independence for all. By prioritizing the development of NLP applications that cater to a spectrum of abilities, technology creators reaffirm a commitment to a society where every individual is afforded the same opportunities to thrive. As this technology evolves, the focus remains constant on enhancing the quality of life for differently-abled individuals, championing a more inclusive and supportive world.

The integration of emotional intelligence into NLP systems heralds a new era of empathetic technology. Such systems are now sophisticated enough to detect nuances in tone, language, and expression, allowing them to respond to human emotions in a thoughtful manner. In customer service, this means virtual assistants can perceive frustration in a customer's voice or word choice and adjust their responses accordingly, perhaps by escalating the issue or altering their tone to one of understanding and patience.

In healthcare, emotionally intelligent NLP systems offer a dual benefit: they assist clinicians by providing insights into a patient's emotional state, thereby informing treatment approaches, and they support patients by offering empathetic communication, particularly when human interaction is limited. These systems can recognize signs of emotional distress in speech patterns and content, allowing for timely intervention.

Emotionally attuned machines can also extend their influence into education, where they can detect students' frustration or confusion, adapting the pace or complexity of content to match the learner's emotional state. This ensures a supportive learning environment that can enhance student engagement and retention.

Moreover, emotionally intelligent NLP systems hold a transformative potential in accessibility technology, providing an empathetic touch to those with different abilities. By understanding emotional cues, these systems can offer more personalized support, thus fostering greater independence for users.

The future of emotionally intelligent NLP is one where technology not only understands what we say but also how we feel, bridging the gap between human and machine interaction and creating a more humane and responsive technological ecosystem.

For organizations to fully harness the benefits of Natural Language Processing, a structured approach is essential. It begins with a thorough assessment of current operations and identifying areas where this technology can have the most significant impact. Subsequently, organizations need to develop a strategy that includes not just adopting this technology but also seamlessly integrating it into existing workflows. This strategy must account for both the technical aspects and the human component of integration, ensuring that the systems are user-friendly and enhance the end-user experience.

A robust strategy for this technology also requires a focus on data governance and the ethical use of technology. It's crucial for organizations to ensure that data for training models are unbiased and that privacy is respected. Ethical considerations are paramount in designing and implementing these systems, especially when they're used in decision-making processes that affect human lives.

Additionally, organizations should prepare for workforce upskilling to proficiently manage these tools. This encompasses not only the technical team but also managerial and executive staff, who need to grasp the capabilities and limits of this technology for informed decision-making.

Embracing this technology involves challenges, but with meticulous planning, ethical foresight, and a commitment to ongoing learning and adaptation, organizations can unlock its transformative potential. This transformation is a continuous journey of evolution, mirroring the advancement of the technology itself. Organizations that adeptly manage this journey will find themselves at the vanguard of innovation, enjoying the benefits of heightened efficiency, better decision-making, and deeper insights.

As we conclude this chapter, we find ourselves on the brink of a new era in human-machine interaction, fundamentally reshaped by the capabilities of this technology. Our exploration through this field of innovation and transformation has given us a thorough understanding of its critical role in improving communication, customer service, and operational efficiency.

The case study of a company that transformed its customer service using language processing technology highlights the significant impact of this technology. It exemplifies how this technology can overcome conventional obstacles, creating experiences that are not only efficient but also empathetic and attuned to human needs. The transformation observed in this organization is a clear indication of the potential of language processing technology in redefining the realms of business and communication.

Throughout the chapter, we have seen diverse aspects of this technology, from its application in customer service and operations to its role in cybersecurity and information management. We observed how systems capable of understanding and processing human language have grown to be more than mere tools; they are collaborators in enabling smooth and intuitive interactions.

Furthermore, we examined the ethical considerations vital to the implementation of this technology. The focus on privacy, bias prevention, and intellectual property rights underscores the necessity for responsible innovation. As language processing technology continues to advance, upholding ethical standards and valuing human principles are critical in realizing its full potential.

Chapter 14
Future-proofing Your NLP

What it would be like if our interactions with machines were as intuitive and responsive as conversations with our fellow humans? Imagine a world where technology not only understands our language but also our intentions and emotions. This is not a glimpse into a distant future but the present reality shaped by the transformative power of Natural Language Processing. In this chapter, we will discuss this evolution, following the story of a company that harnessed NLP to revolutionize customer interactions. As we unravel their journey, we'll witness how NLP transcends the boundaries of technology, creating a seamless blend of efficiency and empathy, and leading to a climax that reshapes our understanding of human-machine interaction.

In considering the long-term scalability of NLP systems, organizations should prioritize flexibility and adaptability. As data volumes expand and user expectations rise, NLP architectures must be designed to handle this growth without performance degradation. It's not merely about ensuring that the system can handle larger datasets, but also that it can integrate new features and capabilities as they become available.

To address scalability, businesses should embrace modular designs in their NLP systems. This allows individual components to be updated or replaced without disrupting the entire system. For example, as language models evolve, a modular system would enable you to integrate the latest models to enhance understanding and generation capabilities without overhauling your entire NLP infrastructure.

Another key aspect is the use of cloud-based services that provide elasticity. Cloud services can dynamically allocate resources based on demand, ensuring that NLP applications remain responsive and efficient regardless of workload spikes. This also aids in controlling costs, as resources can be scaled down during periods of low demand.

Furthermore, organizations should implement robust data management practices. As NLP systems learn and adapt from data, the quality and structure of the data become critical for long-term scalability. Effective data management ensures that as the volume of data grows, its quality and the insights derived from it do not diminish.

Investing in advanced analytics is also vital. These can monitor the performance and usage patterns of NLP applications, providing insights into potential bottlenecks before they become critical issues. By using predictive analytics, organizations can anticipate future demands and make proactive adjustments to their NLP systems.

Finally, considering the human aspect of scalability is essential. As NLP systems become more widespread within an organization, the need for a skilled workforce to manage, maintain, and evolve these systems grows. Therefore, a plan for ongoing education and training is crucial to ensure that your team's skills remain current with the rapid advancements in NLP technology.

In summary, for NLP systems to remain effective and efficient over the long term, they must be built with growth in mind. This means not only technical scalability but also scalability of processes and human resources. Organizations that approach NLP with a forward-looking, holistic strategy will be well-placed to leverage its full potential, no matter how the data or business evolves.

Staying current with technological advancements is not just advantageous—it's imperative for maintaining a competitive edge. The pace at which machine learning and Artificial Intelligence are evolving means that what's cutting-edge today may be obsolete tomorrow. Organizations keen on optimizing their NLP investments must therefore remain vigilant and responsive to technological shifts.

One of the most powerful aspects of these advancements is the ability to process and understand language on a nuanced level. This includes discerning intent, context, and even the subtleties of different dialects or colloquialisms. As machine learning models grow more sophisticated, they can navigate these complexities with increased accuracy, thus broadening the scope of potential applications.

Moreover, new frameworks and tools are continuously emerging, offering streamlined development processes, more efficient algorithms, and enhanced learning capabilities. For instance, transformer models such as BERT and GPT have revolutionized how machines understand human language, making it possible to implement more complex, conversational interfaces across various platforms.

Organizations can leverage these advancements to refine customer service bots, create more effective content analysis tools, or enhance language translation services. The trick lies in remaining agile, being willing to experiment with new frameworks, and not shying away from pivoting when a new technology proves its worth.

Data governance underpins the success of any NLP initiative. It's a multifaceted endeavor, spanning data quality, management, privacy, and compliance with ever-shifting regulations. A robust data governance framework ensures that data, the lifeblood of NLP systems, is handled with the utmost integrity throughout its lifecycle.

Central to this framework is the establishment of clear policies around data usage, storage, and security. This not only safeguards sensitive information but also ensures that the data feeding into your NLP systems is of the highest quality—crucial for the accuracy of outputs.

With regulations like GDPR in Europe and various privacy laws emerging globally, adherence to legal standards is non-negotiable. It's also a matter of trust; customers are increasingly savvy about data privacy, and their willingness to engage with your services will hinge on your reputation for data stewardship.

Data governance is not a one-off project but a continuous commitment. As new data types and sources emerge, the framework must evolve. Regular audits and updates to policies will help maintain compliance and ensure that data governance remains a strategic asset rather than a liability.

Transfer learning has emerged as a cornerstone in the field of NLP, allowing for rapid advancements and application-specific tuning of models. By utilizing pre-trained models, organizations can bypass much of the heavy lifting involved in training from scratch, focusing instead on fine-tuning models to fit their unique requirements.

This approach not only accelerates development cycles but also imbues NLP systems with a wealth of pre-existing knowledge. It allows them to quickly adapt to new contexts and continue learning from there, becoming more specialized and effective in their tasks.

The continuous improvement cycle fostered by transfer learning ensures that NLP systems can stay up-to-date with minimal intervention. As new data becomes available or as language usage patterns evolve, these systems can be incrementally updated, thus maintaining their relevance and accuracy.

Moreover, transfer learning democratizes access to advanced NLP capabilities. Small businesses and startups, which may not have the resources for extensive model training, can now implement sophisticated NLP features, leveling the playing field and fostering innovation.

Agile development methodologies have become indispensable as it pertains to language processing. These methodologies prioritize flexibility, customer feedback, and rapid iteration, which are crucial for the development of NLP systems that are resilient to the fast-paced changes in technology and user needs. With agile practices, NLP projects can be adjusted quickly in response to new insights or shifts in market demands, ensuring that the end product remains relevant and valuable.

The core of agile methodology is its iterative nature, which allows development teams to build NLP applications in small, manageable increments. This approach encourages continuous evaluation and refinement of the project's direction. By testing and releasing in cycles, teams can identify potential issues early and iterate on solutions, reducing the risk of significant problems at later stages.

User feedback is another cornerstone of agile methodologies. In the context of NLP, where understanding and meeting user expectations are critical, gathering and incorporating user feedback helps tailor the system to provide more accurate and user-friendly interactions. This continuous loop of feedback and improvement ensures that NLP systems are not only technically sound but also resonate with the target audience.

Continuous monitoring and maintenance are critical strategies for ensuring the longevity of NLP investments. As language is inherently fluid, with new slang, terminologies, and usage patterns emerging regularly, NLP systems must be able to evolve and adapt. Continuous monitoring allows for the detection of shifts in language and user behavior, prompting timely updates to the system to maintain its effectiveness.

Maintenance of NLP systems is not merely about fixing what's broken but also about enhancing and expanding capabilities to meet emerging needs. Regular updates to NLP models and algorithms are necessary to incorporate new data, address changing contexts, and improve overall performance. This proactive approach prevents the system from becoming outdated, preserving its utility and user satisfaction over time.

A culture of innovation and experimentation is pivotal for the sustainable advancement of NLP technology. It's through this culture that new ideas surface and are transformed into tangible solutions. Organizations that encourage their teams to challenge the status quo and explore uncharted territories in NLP are more likely to develop groundbreaking applications that push the boundaries of what's possible.

Cross-functional collaboration is a key element in this process, bringing together diverse perspectives and expertise to explore complex problems from multiple angles. It's this synergy that can lead to innovative NLP solutions, which might not emerge within more siloed or conservative environments.

Experimentation is also central to this culture. It involves not just the freedom to test new ideas but also the understanding that not all experiments will succeed. By embracing failure as a stepping stone to innovation, organizations can cultivate a resilient mindset that values learning and growth.

These strategies collectively form a robust approach to securing the future of NLP projects. Agile development ensures responsiveness to change, continuous monitoring maintains the relevance of NLP systems, and a culture of innovation drives the pursuit of new frontiers in NLP technology.

To future-proof investments in Natural Language Processing, one must remain well-informed about the latest developments in the field. Engaging with the NLP research community and staying attuned to industry trends are not just beneficial practices, but essential ones. Participation in conferences, symposiums, and workshops, as well as subscriptions to leading journals and publications, can provide insights into the latest research and innovative techniques that are driving the field forward.

Incorporating new research findings into existing NLP systems can significantly enhance their capabilities, providing a competitive edge. For instance, advancements in understanding language nuances and sentiment can be translated into more sophisticated customer service chatbots, offering a more human-like interaction. Similarly, leveraging breakthroughs in machine translation can result in expanding global reach by breaking down language barriers.

Understanding these trends also helps in anticipating shifts in technology, which is paramount for strategic planning and investment. By being proactive, organizations can allocate resources wisely, ensuring they are not left behind as the industry evolves. This forward-thinking approach can also uncover opportunities for innovation, leading to the development of new products or the improvement of existing ones, thereby maintaining relevance and market position.

A diverse and skilled NLP team is a powerhouse for innovation and success. Diversity in a team brings a range of experiences, perspectives, and problem-solving skills. It fosters an environment where creative solutions to complex NLP challenges can emerge. In the context of NLP, diversity is not just cultural or gender-based but also encompasses a variety of academic backgrounds and technical expertise.

Attracting top talent in NLP requires creating an environment that values continuous learning and knowledge sharing. This involves not only offering competitive salaries and benefits but also providing opportunities for professional growth through training and development programs. Encouraging participation in open-source projects or collaborative research can enhance skills and keep the team at the cutting edge of NLP technology.

A skilled NLP team is well-versed in linguistics, computer science, and data analysis. This multi-disciplinary expertise is crucial for tackling the complexities of language processing. For example, understanding the linguistic subtleties of different dialects can be instrumental in developing more accurate speech recognition systems. Similarly, expertise in machine learning is vital for building models that can learn and adapt to new language patterns efficiently.

Adapting to change and embracing disruption is paramount in the dynamic world of NLP. Change is not a barrier but an avenue for progress and innovation. By fostering an agile mindset, organizations can pivot and adapt their NLP strategies to harness new technologies and respond to market changes effectively.

Developing a robust change management framework specific to NLP projects can streamline the adoption of new technologies and methodologies. This framework should include clear communication channels, training programs to upskill employees, and strategies to mitigate any resistance to change. For example, as conversational Artificial Intelligence becomes more advanced, employees must be prepared to work alongside these systems, understanding their capabilities and limitations.

Embracing disruption also means recognizing the potential in emerging technologies that may initially seem disruptive. For instance, the rise of voice search has necessitated the optimization of search algorithms for spoken queries. Companies that anticipated this shift and adapted their SEO strategies accordingly were able to maintain their competitive edge.

As we conclude this chapter, we take a moment to reflect on our journey through the captivating domain of Natural Language Processing and its significant impact on contemporary communication and operations. The narrative of a company that revolutionized customer interaction with this technology stands as a vibrant testament to its transformative capacity. It exemplifies how this technology can seamlessly connect digital processes with human intricacies, boosting efficiency while fostering customer connections.

The central insight from our exploration is the versatility and adaptability of this technology. In roles ranging from enhancing customer service to improving operational efficiency, it emerges as a dynamic entity capable of learning, evolving, and personalizing interactions. Its efficacy in grasping the nuances of human language and sentiment has enabled more human-like interactions with machines.

Our exploration covered various facets of this technology, observing its contribution to streamlining processes, aiding decision-making, and enriching customer experiences. The focus on continuous learning and adaptability within these systems emphasizes the need to stay ahead in an ever-changing technological environment. By leveraging the latest advancements and incorporating them into business practices, organizations can sustain their competitive advantage and continue to innovate.

As this chapter draws to a close, we gain a deeper appreciation for the capabilities of this technology and its potential to redefine our interaction with technology. The process of integrating this technology into different aspects of business and communication is a continuous one, each advancement opening new doors for innovation and connectivity. The future of Natural Language Processing beckons with prospects of even more fluid, intuitive, and empathetic human-machine interactions.

Chapter 15

Emerging NLP Trends Beyond Today

Have you ever imagined a world where technology doesn't just respond to your commands but understands your emotions and context? Picture a future where machines engage with us not as tools, but as empathetic partners in our daily lives. This is not a distant fantasy; it's the reality being shaped by Natural Language Processing. This chapter discusses the transformative power of NLP, illustrating its impact across various sectors. From revolutionizing customer service with responsive chatbots to enhancing healthcare through insightful data analysis.

Natural Language Processing stands at the forefront of the technological revolution, redefining how we interact with machines and process vast amounts of information. Today, NLP technologies permeate various sectors, offering innovative solutions to age-old problems and creating unprecedented efficiencies.

In customer service, NLP facilitates seamless interactions through chatbots and virtual assistants, capable of understanding and processing human language to provide instantaneous and accurate responses. This capability not only enhances customer experience but also streamlines operations, reducing the need for extensive human intervention.

Business analytics has seen NLP algorithms that are capable of sifting through unstructured data—such as customer reviews, social media chatter, and news articles —to extract actionable insights. Companies can, therefore, grasp market sentiments, predict trends, and tailor their strategies accordingly.

The financial industry benefits from NLP in combating fraud and enhancing security. By analyzing transactional language and patterns, NLP systems can detect anomalies indicative of fraudulent activity, thereby bolstering the integrity of financial transactions.

Educationally, NLP has transformed learning experiences by enabling the creation of personalized learning platforms. These platforms adapt to individual learning styles and paces, making education more accessible and effective. Moreover, NLP tools assist in language learning, breaking down barriers and opening doors to global communication.

In healthcare, NLP is a game-changer, improving patient outcomes by extracting meaningful data from clinical notes, which can lead to better diagnosis and treatment plans. It also supports mental health initiatives by analyzing speech patterns that may indicate psychological distress.

The driving forces behind the growth of Natural Language Processing are diverse. Innovations in machine learning, particularly deep learning, have substantially enhanced the technology's ability to interpret context and subtlety in language. Moreover, the growing availability of vast datasets and increased computational power allows for processing language on an unprecedented scale.

As technology continually evolves, this technology remains robust and adaptable, becoming a vital element in the toolkit for innovation. Its applications are varied, and its potential seems limitless. It plays a pivotal role in optimizing workflows and opening new channels of user interaction, acting as a conduit between the complexity of human language and the accuracy of computational processes.

Understanding and utilizing the potential of this technology is essential for any organization striving to remain competitive. It goes beyond mere adoption; it involves strategic integration to enhance capabilities, drive innovation, and foster growth. This epitomizes the power and potential of this technology in today's world, steering us towards a more efficient and connected reality.

The trajectory of this technology is profoundly influenced by the synergy between Artificial Intelligence and machine learning. These technologies have refined its sophistication, enabling machines to process and generate language with increased complexity and nuance. AI and ML algorithms can now contextually interpret language, discern emotional undertones, and create text that resembles human speech.

This is particularly evident in conversational AI, where chatbots and virtual assistants are becoming more nuanced and aware of context. The progression from simple decision-tree based interactions to AI-driven, dynamic conversation models is a significant advancement. These models leverage deep learning to better understand user intentions, allowing for more fluid conversations.

Additionally, the abundance of big data fuels the advancement of this technology by providing the extensive datasets needed for machine learning models to grasp human language. The combination of these large datasets with the processing power of cloud computing enables these systems to analyze language data on a vast scale, crucial for applications like real-time sentiment analysis on social media or instant translation services.

The rise of cloud-based services in this field has made advanced language processing accessible to businesses of all sizes, without the need for substantial investment in computational infrastructure. These scalable solutions can adapt to changing needs, ensuring that applications remain cutting-edge and cost-effective.

With the increase in global business and community interactions, the demand for multilingual language processing is growing. Effortless communication across different languages is a key competitive advantage in the global market. Leading the charge in this area are machine translation services and cross-language information retrieval systems, breaking down language barriers.

A significant challenge is developing systems that accurately interpret and translate linguistic nuances, idioms, and cultural contexts across multiple languages. This requires not only extensive bilingual or multilingual datasets but also advanced machine learning models capable of understanding the subtleties of various languages. Innovations in this area include neural machine translation systems, which use deep neural networks to enhance translation quality by understanding entire sentences rather than mere phrases.

Another important development is cross-language information retrieval, which enables the search and extraction of information across different languages. This is particularly valuable for global businesses needing to monitor brand sentiment in various regions and languages. These translation systems are trained to not only translate but also maintain the sentiment and context of the original text, enabling more accurate global data analysis.

The expansion of multilingual language processing also has profound implications for social inclusion. It allows speakers of less common languages to access technology and information that was previously unavailable in their native languages. This democratization of language technology is creating a more inclusive digital world where language is no longer a barrier to information or communication.

These trends underscore the ongoing evolution of this technology as a transformative force in global communication, business analytics, and social inclusion. By embracing these developments, businesses and individuals can strategically position themselves in a world where language technology is a key facet of progress and connectivity.

Context-aware NLP systems represent a significant leap forward in technology's ability to interact with humans. These systems harness contextual data—previous interactions, time of day, location, and even the user's tone of voice—to grasp the user's intent more accurately. By integrating these cues, NLP applications can offer responses that are not only relevant but also anticipate the user's needs, leading to more meaningful and efficient exchanges.

For instance, when a user asks a virtual assistant to "set a meeting," context-aware systems can infer specifics such as the usual meeting time preferences or the regular participants based on past behavior. Beyond scheduling, context-aware NLP transforms search engines into intelligent agents that consider user history and preferences to deliver personalized results.

Personalization in NLP extends to content delivery and recommendation systems. Streaming services, e-commerce platforms, and news aggregators utilize NLP to analyze user preferences and behavior, providing tailored content that aligns with individual tastes and interests. By doing so, they not only increase user engagement but also foster loyalty and satisfaction.

However, this level of personalization raises critical ethical questions about privacy and data security. Users are increasingly aware of the value and sensitivity of their personal data. NLP systems, therefore, must navigate the fine line between personalization and privacy. Responsible use of data, transparency about how data is collected and used, and adherence to stringent data protection standards are non-negotiable elements in the design of context-aware NLP systems.

Developers and businesses need to be acutely aware of the potential for bias in personalized content delivered by NLP systems. This can inadvertently lead to the reinforcement of echo chambers, where users are exposed only to information that aligns with their existing beliefs and preferences. Therefore, the ethical design of these systems is critical and should incorporate mechanisms that ensure diversity and fairness in content recommendations. Addressing these concerns is not just a technical challenge but a moral imperative.

Navigating the ethical considerations of Natural Language Processing is as nuanced and intricate as the technology itself. As these systems increasingly become part of our everyday lives, ensuring they operate justly and beneficially for society is essential. A key aspect of this journey is acknowledging that these algorithms, like all AI forms, can inherit and amplify biases from their training data. Such biases can result in discriminatory outcomes, affecting people differently based on gender, race, and other personal characteristics. Recognizing and addressing these biases is crucial for developing technologies that are not only advanced but also equitable and responsible.

Developers and stakeholders bear the important duty of auditing datasets and algorithms for bias. This process is not a one-off task but an ongoing commitment requiring vigilance as language and societal norms change. Techniques like adversarial testing can reveal hidden biases by challenging systems with complex inputs.

Transparency in these systems is another critical ethical aspect. Demystifying how systems make decisions, especially in complex models like deep neural networks, is challenging. Efforts towards explainable AI are crucial to make the decision-making process of these models more comprehensible, building trust among users and stakeholders.

Accountability in these scenarios is equally important. When these systems are used in high-stakes situations, such as predicting criminal behavior or screening job applicants, errors can have significant consequences. Establishing clear guidelines for accountability ensures that there is a framework for redress and improvement when things go wrong.

Privacy and data protection are crucial, particularly as these systems often process sensitive personal data. Compliance with data protection laws like the GDPR in Europe and various global privacy standards is vital. This adherence is not just about avoiding legal issues; it's about respecting individual rights and maintaining public trust.

Developing and deploying these technologies ethically requires the involvement of diverse stakeholders, including ethicists, sociologists, and the communities impacted by these applications. By incorporating a wide range of perspectives, these technologies can be steered towards outcomes that are fair and beneficial for all society segments. This ethical framework aims to shape an inclusive future where these technologies positively impact society and reflect human values' diversity.

The next significant advancement in this field is integrating emotional intelligence into these systems. This step represents a significant evolution in human-computer interaction. Advancements in this technology are now moving towards recognizing and responding to human emotion subtleties. With sentiment analysis and emotion detection, these systems are becoming adept at identifying and interpreting emotions, paving the way for more empathetic and personalized communication.

The applications of emotionally intelligent systems are extensive. In mental health, they can offer support by detecting distress signals in speech or text. In customer service, they can discern customer moods, enhancing service quality.

However, this potential comes with a responsibility to carefully consider ethical aspects. There's a fine line between offering support and invasive surveillance. Emotionally intelligent systems must respect privacy and uphold consent, ensuring individuals control their emotional data. Cultural sensitivity is vital, as emotional expressions vary globally, and systems must recognize these differences to avoid misunderstandings.

Additionally, training these systems requires extensive emotionally annotated language datasets, which must be collected and used without compromising personal privacy. This process involves meticulous curation to avoid perpetuating stereotypes and biases present in the source material.

The design of emotionally intelligent NLP systems requires a multi-disciplinary approach, drawing on insights from psychology, cognitive science, and anthropology to deeply understand emotional expressions. This comprehensive understanding is crucial for NLP systems to advance in a way that truly benefits users, ensuring that these systems can interpret and respond to human emotions with nuanced accuracy.

This multi-disciplinary and holistic approach in NLP development is also paving the way for transformative applications in other sectors, such as healthcare. The integration of NLP into healthcare marks the beginning of a new era where clinical decision-making is significantly enhanced and expedited. NLP's prowess in interpreting and organizing unstructured data, such as physicians' notes, patient records, and medical literature, into actionable insights, revolutionizes patient care. This technology not only simplifies administrative tasks but also plays a crucial role in diagnosing and treating patients. By quickly providing relevant information, NLP systems in healthcare settings can improve both the efficiency and accuracy of medical care.

One of the most notable applications is in the analysis of electronic health records (EHRs). NLP can sift through extensive amounts of data to identify pertinent patient information, which can be crucial for chronic disease management, where monitoring subtle changes over time is critical. Similarly, in mental health, NLP can evaluate patient language and speech patterns to assist in the diagnosis and monitoring of conditions like depression and anxiety.

In medical research, NLP facilitates the extraction of insights from vast databases of scientific literature, helping researchers stay updated with the latest findings without having to manually review each document. This accelerates the pace of medical discovery and the development of new treatments.

Another innovative use of NLP in healthcare is through chatbots and virtual health assistants. These tools provide immediate responses to patient inquiries, schedule appointments, and can even offer preliminary medical advice based on symptoms described by the user, thereby improving healthcare accessibility and patient engagement.

Despite these benefits, the application of NLP in healthcare is not without its challenges. Paramount among these is the safeguarding of sensitive patient data. Any NLP system handling health information must comply with stringent regulations such as HIPAA in the United States. Furthermore, data security protocols must be robust to protect against breaches that could compromise patient privacy.

Another hurdle is ensuring the accuracy and reliability of NLP systems in clinical settings. Misinterpretations of medical jargon or patient information can have serious implications. Thus, continuous validation and oversight by healthcare professionals are vital.

Finally, there is the challenge of interoperability. Healthcare systems are often siloed, and NLP applications must be able to seamlessly integrate across different platforms and data formats to be truly effective.

Natural Language Processing extends beyond commercial applications to address critical societal challenges. It serves as a potent tool for social good, with its capacity to analyze vast quantities of data for insightful and potentially life-saving applications.

One of the most significant roles NLP plays is in the detection and mitigation of disinformation. In an era where facts are often obscured by falsehoods, NLP technologies can sift through online content to identify and flag fake news. By analyzing writing styles, cross-referencing facts, and tracking the spread of information, NLP systems can alert platforms and users to potential misinformation, thus preserving the integrity of public discourse.

Public Health sees contributions in the form of social welfare by monitoring social media and other digital platforms for emerging public health crises. For example, by detecting shifts in public sentiment or increases in discussions around certain symptoms, health organizations can anticipate outbreaks and mobilize resources more rapidly.

NLP also plays a pivotal role in disaster response. By quickly parsing through social media posts, NLP systems can locate people in need during a disaster, identify the most critical needs, and optimize the response of aid organizations. Such real-time data processing can be the difference between life and death in emergency situations.

Moreover, NLP aids in humanitarian efforts by breaking down language barriers. Translating between languages and dialects, NLP helps disseminate crucial information across linguistic divides, ensuring that aid reaches those who need it without language being an impediment.

Accessibility is another area where NLP is making a tangible impact. For individuals with disabilities, NLP-driven tools can translate spoken language into text or sign language, bridging communication gaps and fostering inclusivity.

However, the deployment of NLP for social good is not without challenges. Ethical use of data is a concern, with privacy considerations at the forefront. Ensuring that NLP solutions are used ethically and responsibly, with the consent of those whose data is being analyzed, is critical.

The trajectory of NLP is veering towards an era where multimodal interactions with machines will become commonplace. This evolution marks a shift from text-based engagements to more dynamic, multimodal experiences where voice, visuals, and even haptics are integrated seamlessly.

Voice-activated systems have made significant strides, moving from simple command-response interactions to sophisticated dialogue exchanges. Today's virtual assistants are capable of understanding nuances in speech, discerning emotions, and providing contextually relevant responses. This progress in voice NLP is not only about understanding words but grasping the speaker's intent, which requires a machine learning approach that can interpret tone, inflection, and even pauses.

Visual NLP is another burgeoning area, where Artificial Intelligence interprets and generates information from images and videos. This includes understanding the content of an image, the sentiment of a video, or the actions within it. For example, visual NLP can analyze medical imagery to assist in diagnostics, or review surveillance footage for security purposes.

Multimodal NLP, which combines text, voice, and visuals, offers even more potential. By processing multiple types of input, Artificial Intelligence systems can provide richer, more accurate interactions. Consider a scenario where a user asks a virtual assistant for help with a physical task; the system could assess the spoken words, the environment's visuals, and other sensory data to provide precise, step-by-step assistance.

The implications of these technologies extend to numerous fields. In education, multimodal NLP could lead to more engaging learning platforms that adapt to a student's learning style, whether they are auditory, visual, or kinesthetic learners. For businesses, it can mean customer support that not only hears but sees and understands the issues customers face, providing more empathetic and effective service.

As with any technological advancement, challenges persist, particularly around ensuring privacy and security in systems that process such diverse and personal data. Additionally, there is the need for robust, inclusive datasets to train these systems, avoiding biases that could skew their understanding and output.

The intersection of academic research and industrial application has been a fertile ground for NLP advancements. This partnership has fueled innovations that are rapidly transforming the way we interact with machines and how they understand us.

Academic researchers have long been at the forefront of NLP, pushing the boundaries of what's possible with language understanding and generation. They publish papers that often form the theoretical backbone of NLP advancements, exploring complex models and algorithms. These academic pursuits, however, need the industry's practical focus and resources to transition from theory to application.

Industry players bring to the table real-world data, infrastructure, and application scenarios that are critical for testing and refining academic theories. Companies like Google, Amazon, and Microsoft have been instrumental in taking NLP research from the lab to the living room, integrating it into products used by millions.

This synergy is evident in the development of transformer models, which have revolutionized NLP in recent years. Models like BERT, GPT, and others have their roots in academia but were developed further by industry, leading to breakthroughs in machine translation, sentiment analysis, and more. Such models have achieved unprecedented understanding of context, grammar, and semantics.

Industry collaboration also provides academia with the unique feedback loop of user interaction data, which is invaluable for iterative improvement. Additionally, the industry's financial and computational resources allow for the training of models at a scale often unattainable by academic institutions alone.

However, challenges in this collaboration exist, such as aligning academic curiosity with business objectives, intellectual property rights, and the ethics of NLP applications. But the benefits far outweigh the challenges. By leveraging each other's strengths, academia and industry can accelerate the pace of innovation, ensuring NLP systems become more intelligent, reliable, and integrated into our daily lives.

Looking ahead, maintaining this collaborative momentum is crucial. As NLP systems become more embedded in critical sectors like healthcare, law, and education, the need for robust, ethical, and advanced language processing technology becomes more apparent. This partnership is not just about advancing technology; it's about shaping the future of communication and information exchange.

In this chapter, we have looked at how we interact with machines and process information with the help of NLP. Natural language process has emerged not just as a technological tool but as a transformative force, redefining the boundaries of human-computer interaction. Its ability to understand, interpret, and respond to human language in a contextually aware and emotionally intelligent manner signifies a paradigm shift towards a more intuitive and responsive technological future.

Through diverse applications, from enhancing customer experiences to streamlining business operations, and from advancing healthcare to enriching educational experiences, NLP demonstrates its versatility and indispensability. Its role in enabling machines to decipher the complexities of human language and emotion underscores a move towards more empathetic and personalized technology.

Moreover, this chapter underscored the importance of continuous innovation, ethical considerations, and data governance in the evolution of NLP. Embracing these principles ensures that NLP technologies not only advance in capabilities but also align with societal values and individual needs.

In essence, NLP stands at the intersection of human ingenuity and artificial intelligence, promising a future where enhanced communication and understanding lead to richer, more meaningful interactions. As we continue to explore and harness the potential of NLP, we move closer to a world where technology comprehends not just our words, but also the intentions and emotions behind them, fostering a more harmonious and efficient coexistence with the digital world.

Chapter 16

Conversations Beyond Borders With NLP

Imagine entering a room filled with people from every corner of the world, each speaking a different language. Now, imagine understanding every word, every nuance, every emotion behind their words as if they were speaking your native language. This is the transformative power of Natural Language Processing.

In this chapter, we will look at the dynamic relationship of language technology, examining how it connects different languages and enhances worldwide communication. We examine a case study of an international corporation employing this technology to manage the intricacies of multilingual customer interactions, hinting at the significant influence this innovation has in bridging linguistic gaps and promoting universal comprehension.

Multilingual data embodies the rich tapestry of human communication. Each language serves not just as a mode of communication but as a vessel of cultural and contextual significance. This complexity is compounded when developing NLP systems that aim to serve users across the globe. The task extends beyond mere translation—it requires an understanding of idioms, colloquialisms, and the subtle ways context shapes meaning. For instance, sentiment analysis in one language may not directly translate to another due to these nuanced differences. Recognizing these challenges is the first step in building effective multilingual NLP systems that are both accurate and culturally sensitive.

Developing models that can navigate the linguistic multitude of languages necessitates strategies that both differentiate and unify. Techniques like multilingual embeddings can capture semantic similarities across languages, enabling a single model to operate in various linguistic environments. Furthermore, employing a universal sentence encoder that understands the sentence structures shared across languages can streamline the training process. These strategies focus on exploiting the commonalities among languages while also fine-tuning for linguistic idiosyncrasies. Thus, they form the backbone of creating versatile NLP systems capable of serving a global user base.

The foundation of any robust NLP system is its dataset. As we talk abouty multilingual NLP, collecting and annotating datasets is a formidable endeavor. This process must ensure diversity in linguistic representation, including low-resource languages often underrepresented in technology. Collaborating with native speakers and linguists is essential to capture the essence of each language in the data. Annotating this data requires meticulous attention to maintain consistency and accuracy across different languages. By surmounting these data-related hurdles, the groundwork is laid for NLP systems that can truly understand and engage with users worldwide.

As we continue our path ahead in the development of multilingual NLP, these considerations become pillars upon which more inclusive and globally aware systems are built. The vision is to foster seamless communication and understanding, bridging language barriers with technology that is not only technically proficient but also culturally attuned.

Cross-language information retrieval (CLIR) systems serve as linguistic conduits, facilitating the flow of knowledge across the barriers of language. A user's inquiry, phrased in one language, is met with information from a trove of content in another, thanks to the intricate mechanisms of translation and semantic recognition embedded within these systems. The process isn't merely translational but interpretative—requiring the system to grasp the nuances of the query's context, cultural underpinnings, and possible ambiguities.

Achieving this involves leveraging computational linguistics and machine learning. For instance, when a user queries in English for scholarly articles on "sustainable energy," a CLIR system will interpret the request, translate it, and pull relevant documents in German, Mandarin, or any number of other languages, all the while ensuring the thematic essence of "sustainability" and "energy" remains intact. This multilingual bridge is not just a technical marvel but a facilitator of cross-cultural research and collaboration, removing silos that have long hindered the seamless exchange of knowledge.

The process of classifying and linking documents across languages is a complex task, akin to finding patterns in a cosmic web where each thread is a different hue. Cross-lingual document embeddings are at the forefront of this challenge, which translates documents into numerical vectors representing their semantic content. This numerical representation allows for language-agnostic comparisons—documents from different language corpora can be mapped in the same semantic space, revealing similarities that transcend linguistic boundaries.

Such techniques power applications that range from global news aggregation, where articles on the same event but in different languages are clustered, to customer service, where similar queries can be identified and addressed in a unified manner, irrespective of the language of origination. The core of this innovation lies in the ability to distill the essence of texts, to see beyond the words to the meaning they convey, and to group them in a way that illuminates their underlying connections.

The intricacies of language and the subtle cues of culture form a complex tapestry that cross-lingual information retrieval systems must navigate with precision. The variances are not just in vocabulary or grammar but in the way concepts are constructed and communicated. For example, a phrase steeped in cultural significance in one language may have no direct translation in another, requiring the system to understand and convey the concept rather than the literal words.

The intricate complexity of language, with its idiomatic expressions, colloquialisms, and language-specific puns, demands a complete understanding of cultural contexts for accurate interpretation. Overcoming these challenges requires a multidisciplinary approach, blending computational methods with cultural and linguistic insights. Such an approach ensures that systems can navigate the subtleties of human language and the richness of cultural expressions. As these systems evolve, they are poised to become more than just tools for communication; they are emerging as conduits for cultural empathy and understanding, weaving the diverse tapestry of human languages into a more interconnected world.

As Natural language processing evolves, it will be exemplified by the remarkable advancements in Machine Translation, particularly in Neural Machine Translation. (NMT) is redefining the capabilities of translation technology, transcending the role of a mere substitute for human translation to become a sophisticated tool in bridging language barriers.

Unlike its predecessors, NMT goes beyond word-for-word translation; it comprehends entire sentences, grasps contextual nuances, and often delivers translations with a remarkable level of fluency. This technology operates as a comprehensive neural network, modeling the entire translation process. NMT's advancement symbolizes a significant stride in the journey towards more nuanced and effective cross-lingual communication, aligning with the goal of fostering a deeper understanding and connection across different languages and cultures.

The essence of these advancements is the ability of NMT to learn from vast amounts of bilingual text data. This has been facilitated further by recent innovations like transformer models, which eschew the sequential processing of traditional neural networks for a parallel approach, significantly improving speed and efficiency. Attention mechanisms within these models allow the system to focus on specific parts of the source text when predicting a word, much like a human translator would. This has led to translations that are not just grammatically correct but are contextually nuanced and culturally relevant.

Expressions and idioms are the soul of a language, often defying literal translation. For machine translation systems, they present a unique challenge, as the meaning is not always evident from the individual words. These language-specific intricacies require an understanding that spans beyond vocabulary and grammar to include culture and context.

Recent advancements in machine translation involve context-aware models capable of considering not just individual words or phrases, but entire sentences and surrounding paragraphs. This approach allows for a more nuanced understanding of idioms and expressions, often requiring the system to cross-reference vast datasets or be trained on bilingual texts rich in cultural content. The aim here is not merely to translate words but to preserve the essence of the original phrase, ensuring that it is not only understandable but also resonant for the target audience. Such an approach signifies a move towards translations that are not just linguistically accurate but culturally attuned.

At the core of these advanced translation systems are neural networks, which are fundamental in modeling the complex patterns found in human language. These networks are adept at capturing the nuances and intricacies of language, a task essential for effective translation. Recurrent Neural Networks (RNNs), known for their feedback loops, have been pivotal in managing sequential word processing. Meanwhile, transformer models represent a more recent architectural innovation. These models move away from recurrence and instead utilize self-attention mechanisms to assess the influence of different words within a sentence. This shift in technology highlights the continuous evolution of machine translation systems, from understanding basic linguistic structures to grasping the more subtle and complex aspects of human communication.

The utilization of neural networks allows for the integration of linguistic knowledge into the models. For instance, incorporating an understanding of morphology, syntax, and even semantics can refine the quality of translation. By training these networks on a diverse set of languages and dialects, machine translation systems become robust, capable of handling a wide range of linguistic phenomena, from simple sentences to complex discourses.

Each of these advancements is not just an isolated triumph but a synergistic component that propels NLP forward. As machine translation becomes more advanced, it deepens the integration of NLP into global communication, commerce, and cooperation, reinforcing the importance of linguistic inclusivity in our increasingly connected world.

Sentiment analysis ventures into the world of detecting nuances in opinions and emotions. When this is applied to multiple languages, the complexity magnifies. Each language brings its set of emotional expressions, which may not have direct equivalents in others. To build models that can discern sentiment across different languages, we must train them with a diverse range of linguistic data, encompassing various emotional contexts and expressions. This enables the models to not just translate words, but also to convey the underlying sentiment, providing valuable insights into global consumer behavior and public opinion.

Cultural and linguistic diversity presents a multitude of challenges for sentiment analysis. What may be a positive expression in one culture could be neutral or even negative in another. Moreover, the same language can have different dialects and colloquialisms, each with its unique sentiment expressions. Developing sentiment analysis models that can universally understand these variations requires detailed linguistic research and cultural knowledge. These models must be sensitive to context, local dialects, slang, and even non-verbal cues that are transcribed, such as emojis or punctuation, to truly grasp the sentiment being expressed.

Transfer learning has emerged as a solution to the dearth of annotated sentiment data in multiple languages. By adapting a sentiment analysis model trained in one language (typically with abundant data, like English) to understand another, we can expedite the training process and circumvent the scarcity of labeled datasets. This is achieved by retaining the learned parameters and only fine-tuning the model on a smaller set of target language data. This method relies on the universal aspects of sentiment expression across languages, allowing the model to apply its understanding of sentiment in one language to another, thereby enabling the model to perform sentiment analysis across various languages with a level of accuracy previously unattainable.

The integration of advanced components in NLP systems is crucial for global digital platforms. This integration facilitates nuanced customer insights, allows for the localization of products and services, and enhances global communication. As technology progresses, the ability to accurately analyze sentiment across different languages is becoming more than just a technological feat; it's evolving into a vital bridge for deeper understanding in a diverse world. Recognizing the significance of every voice in every language is not just a goal but a necessity in our interconnected global community.

Building on this necessity, multilingual NLP is taking a leap forward by incorporating multiple data modalities, leading to systems that grasp not just words, but various aspects of human expression. These systems integrate text, speech, images, and videos to process and understand different forms of communication. For example, consider a scenario where a user asks a question about a landmark by pointing their smartphone at it, such as, 'What's the news about this place?' In response, the NLP system comprehends the spoken query, recognizes the visual input, and provides relevant news in the user's preferred language. This comprehensive approach breaks down traditional language barriers, fostering seamless interaction on a global scale and enhancing our ability to communicate and access information in increasingly dynamic ways.

The synergy of different modalities requires sophisticated techniques to merge disparate types of data. Cross-modal embeddings are a key technique, creating a shared space where text, speech, image, and video data can be compared and combined. Deep learning architectures such as Convolutional Neural Networks (CNNs) for images and videos, and Recurrent Neural Networks (RNNs) for text and speech, work in tandem to process and interpret this multi-faceted data. These methods help systems to not just process language in isolation but to understand the interplay between different communicative elements, making NLP more intuitive and effective.

Ultimantly, the goal of multimodal multilingual NLP is to elevate user experience, breaking down the silos between different forms of communication. By recognizing spoken language, interpreting visual cues, and understanding contextual videos, these systems offer a more natural and immersive way for users to interact with technology. This is especially transformative in multilingual contexts where users can interact in their native language, with the system understanding and responding appropriately across different modalities. For example, a user can give voice commands to a device to show products in a video, and the system can provide information in the user's language, understanding both the content of the video and the spoken request. This convergence of modalities and languages holds the promise of making technology truly universal, adaptable, and personal to each user's linguistic and cultural context.

By advancing in these multifaceted areas of NLP, we are not just expanding the capabilities of machines; we are paving the way for a future where technology can embrace and respond to the full spectrum of human expression. This isn't limited to the dominant languages or the most common modes of communication; it's about inclusivity and accessibility across all linguistic and cultural boundaries. This integration represents more than a mere technological leap in NLP; it's a step towards a more interconnected and accessible global community.

However, this vision faces challenges, particularly for languages with limited computational resources. In such cases, the scarcity of data can be a significant barrier to NLP development. Yet, innovative strategies like transfer learning offer transformative solutions. Here, models developed for one language are adapted to function with another, overcoming data limitations. Unsupervised learning techniques, which operate without the need for extensively labeled datasets, and semi-supervised methods that combine a small amount of labeled data with larger volumes of unlabeled data, are proving to be game-changers. These approaches, along with creative data augmentation strategies, are expanding the reach of NLP capabilities to these under-resourced languages, thereby enhancing digital inclusivity.

Moreover, languages with intricate morphological structures, like Arabic or Finnish, pose distinct challenges for Natural Language Processing. Comprehending these languages goes beyond word translation; it necessitates grasping complex word formations and meanings. Specialized algorithms for morphological analysis are vital for dissecting and interpreting the varied forms a word can assume in these languages. Additionally, disambiguation algorithms are key to determining the correct interpretation of a word in its specific context. Customizing models to process these complexities is crucial for achieving a more refined and accurate comprehension of these linguistically rich languages, advancing our aim of creating a truly inclusive and comprehensive digital linguistic environment.

Dialects and regional language variations introduce additional layers of complexity. Each dialect can have unique idioms, slang, and pronunciation differences, making a universal approach ineffective. Developing robust systems for this diversity entails gathering dialect-specific data, a challenging yet essential task for model precision. Linguistic expertise is crucial to ensure applications can understand the subtleties and maintain the cultural richness of regional speech.

By mastering these aspects, systems become more inclusive and representative of global linguistic diversity. These advancements not only enhance technology's understanding and interaction with humans but also empower communities by bringing their languages and dialects into the digital space. This endeavor is more than a technical challenge; it's a step towards closing the digital gap and enhancing worldwide communication.

Cultural sensitivity is critical, as languages are imbued with cultural meanings. For effective functioning, systems must recognize cultural nuances to prevent misinterpretation. This involves integrating cultural knowledge into algorithms, ensuring responses are not just linguistically correct but also culturally appropriate. Thus, systems become capable of serving a global audience with respect for cultural diversity, offering more personalized and accurate interactions.

Cultural context influences language use and interpretation. Effective multilingual systems must therefore account for cultural norms and contexts. This goes beyond literal translation to accurately capture the essence of idiomatic expressions and cultural references. Such cultural attunement can improve the relevance and effectiveness of systems across different regions, ensuring they align with users' cultural contexts and expectations.

The interweaving of cultural sensitivity within NLP is not just an added feature; it's a necessity for the technology to be genuinely global. By integrating cultural intelligence into multilingual NLP systems, we not only improve functionality but also foster a respectful and inclusive digital ecosystem that reflects the rich tapestry of human cultures. This attention to cultural details ensures that NLP applications are not only technically proficient but also culturally competent, facilitating better and more meaningful communication across borders.

Bias and stereotypes in NLP can lead to flawed insights and discriminatory outcomes. Ensuring diversity in training datasets is critical for building equitable systems. Techniques such as algorithmic audits for bias detection and the inclusion of anti-bias measures during model training help mitigate these issues. This is not just about fairness; it is also about building trust with users from diverse backgrounds and ensuring that NLP applications serve as tools for inclusion.

The capability for real-time conversation across languages stands at the forefront of NLP's transformative impact on global communication. Real-time communication tools are evolving to support dynamic, instantaneous dialogue, transcending language boundaries. Such tools integrate ASR to transcribe speech into text and then apply machine translation for instant cross-lingual communication. Their importance is profound in today's interconnected society, where the ability to converse without language barriers is invaluable for personal and professional growth.

ASR has undergone a revolution with the incorporation of neural networks, enhancing its ability to discern words amidst various accents and intonations. When combined with simultaneous translation, it paves the way for real-time, natural language conversion. This duality of recognizing spoken words and rendering them in another language instantaneously is an area where NLP showcases its agility. The implications for education, accessibility, and diplomacy are significant, allowing for interactions that were once hindered by language gaps.

Eliminating language barriers is instrumental in uniting global stakeholders. Real-time multilingual communication equips individuals and organizations with the means to collaborate without the hindrance of language differences. This technology is pivotal for international business, enabling negotiations and partnerships to flow more smoothly. It is equally transformative for social and cultural exchanges, allowing for more profound mutual understanding and respect. This seamless interaction across linguistic divides fosters a more inclusive and cooperative international community.

In essence, real-time multilingual communication is a cornerstone in the architecture of global interaction. By equipping NLP systems with the ability to understand, translate, and convey spoken language in real-time, we are not just enhancing communication but reshaping the dynamics of international relations, business, and cultural exchange. This is NLP at its most integrative, demonstrating the harmonization of linguistic diversity in service of a more connected world.

Customization of NLP models to fit distinct domains is critical, more so in multilingual contexts where domain-specific jargon and cultural context significantly influence understanding. For instance, legal and healthcare fields have specialized terminologies that vary by language, requiring models to be fine-tuned with domain-specific datasets. This ensures precision and relevance in NLP tasks such as document classification, information extraction, and question-answering systems across languages. The goal is to build models that not only translate but also interpret the domain-specific context accurately.

Domain adaptation in multilingual settings involves complex dynamics due to the need to transfer knowledge across not just domains but also languages, each with unique linguistic and cultural idiosyncrasies. Transfer learning becomes a strategic approach here, using models pre-trained on large datasets and adapting them to specific domains and languages. This requires innovative techniques to adjust for differences in syntax, semantics, and pragmatics. Overcoming these challenges is key to enabling NLP systems to function with high accuracy and cultural competence across various professional fields.

Harnessing domain-specific resources is pivotal for enhancing multilingual NLP applications. For example, legal documents in English and Spanish may require different emphasis on certain legal terminologies and concepts, which necessitates curated datasets and expert linguistic input for each language. Tapping into such specialized resources aids in building systems that are both linguistically adept and domain-aware. This involves collaborating with subject-matter experts and linguists to annotate data, create lexicons, and simulate real-world scenarios, thus enriching NLP models with the depth of knowledge they need to perform effectively across multiple languages.

Domain-specific multilingual NLP represents a fusion of linguistic mastery and industry-specific expertise. Its complexity lies not just in decoding words and phrases but in understanding their significance within a specific domain's context. This specialized approach is what empowers NLP to offer nuanced, accurate, and actionable insights in a world where expertise transcends linguistic barriers. This evolution towards models that are both multilingual and multidimensional in their understanding and application marks a significant milestone in the field of NLP.

Building on this foundation, multilingual NLP stands at the threshold of a new era, one characterized by a remarkable expansion in language inclusion. This evolution will take us beyond processing the major world languages to embracing regional and indigenous languages, acknowledging the rich tapestry of global linguistic diversity. The upcoming phase is poised to witness an innovative integration of various modalities—melding text with speech, visuals, and videos—to enhance the depth and richness of language processing. Imagine an NLP system that can analyze a news broadcast by interpreting the spoken words, on-screen text, and visual cues, thereby understanding and conveying the message across multiple languages. This integration enables a more comprehensive understanding of content, capturing nuances that a single modality might miss.

Furthermore, there are exciting advancements on the horizon for NLP systems that go beyond mere language comprehension. These future systems aim to detect and interpret underlying emotions, paving the way for empathetic and culturally sensitive communication. Such advancements are not just about technological innovation; they represent a significant step towards creating NLP applications that can truly resonate with users across different cultures, enhancing global connectivity and understanding through more nuanced and empathetic language processing.

Machine learning, particularly AI, is the powerhouse propelling multilingual NLP forward. With machine learning at the forefront, we're witnessing a paradigm shift where models learn from vast amounts of data to recognize patterns and nuances of languages. The next frontier includes self-supervised learning, where systems become adept at learning with minimal human intervention, making the addition of new languages less resource-intensive. These advancements are not merely technical feats; they represent a bridge to universal understanding, enabling instant, accurate communication across the world's tapestry of languages.

As multilingual NLP systems become more pervasive, their deployment comes with a weight of ethical responsibility. Developers and researchers are tasked with ensuring these systems protect individual privacy, treat data with the utmost respect, and represent all users fairly. This involves designing systems that do not perpetuate stereotypes or amplify societal biases, which is particularly challenging given the subtleties of cultural context that can be embedded within language data. By incorporating ethical practices and standards into the development lifecycle, such as transparency in data use and striving for equity in language representation, multilingual NLP can be a force for good, fostering understanding and equity on a global scale.

We we conclude this chapter, we will highlight the fact that natural language processing is a field that stands at the confluence of technology, linguistics, and cultural understanding. We've seen how NLP bridges the divides between languages, bringing down barriers that have long hindered seamless global communication. From the nuances of sentiment analysis in diverse languages to the real-time translation that allows for immediate cross-cultural dialogue, NLP emerges as a pivotal force in the global digital era.

The journey of the international corporation, as unfolded in our case study, epitomizes the transformative impact of NLP. It highlights how businesses can harness this technology to navigate the complexities of multilingual customer interactions, thereby widening their global reach and fostering deeper connections with customers from varied linguistic backgrounds.

Moreover, the ethical considerations, the challenges of incorporating cultural nuances, and the need for ongoing innovation in NLP underscore the complexity and dynamism of this field. As we embrace NLP in its myriad applications, we step into a future where language no longer serves as a barrier but as a bridge connecting people, cultures, and ideas.

Thus, the idea of NLP is one of continuous evolution, a journey towards creating a world where understanding transcends linguistic boundaries, enabling more empathetic and effective communication across the globe. In this interconnected world, NLP stands as a testament to human ingenuity, a tool that not only deciphers words but also unites worlds.

Chapter 17

Bridging Minds and Machine

How will the emerging fusion of Natural Language Processing and Artificial Intelligence redefine our interaction with technology and each other?

This chapter looks into a world where the boundaries between human intelligence and artificial intellect blur, revealing a future sculpted by words understood not just by humans, but also by machines.

Imagine a reality where your spoken words hold the power to control your surroundings, where machines comprehend and respond with an empathy that rivals human understanding. This is not a distant dream but a burgeoning reality, as NLP and AI converge to create a symphony of intelligent interaction.

The amalgamation of Natural Language Processing and Artificial Intelligence is a pioneering step in technological evolution. This partnership transcends traditional boundaries, ushering in an era where machines not only comprehend but also interact with human language in a nuanced manner. AI's contribution to NLP is monumental, particularly in enhancing the understanding and generation of natural language. This has led to the development of AI models that are adept at processing complex linguistic structures and contextual nuances, enabling machines to engage in more meaningful and human-like conversations. The fusion of AI with NLP has also given rise to more intuitive user interfaces and sophisticated language processing tools, significantly impacting fields like customer service and content creation.

The integration of AI in NLP has enabled the creation of advanced machine translation systems. These systems are capable of translating texts and spoken words with an accuracy and fluency that closely mimic human translators. This advancement not only facilitates communication across different languages but also helps in bridging cultural gaps. AI-driven NLP technologies have also made significant strides in sentiment analysis, enabling businesses and organizations to gain deeper insights into consumer behavior and preferences. By analyzing large volumes of data from social media, reviews, and other sources, these systems can accurately gauge public sentiment, assisting in more informed decision-making processes.

Moreover, AI enhances NLP's ability to automate and streamline various tasks, from data extraction to summarization. This capability is particularly beneficial in sectors like legal and healthcare, where handling large volumes of data is a daily occurrence. AI-driven NLP tools can quickly sift through documents, extract relevant information, and summarize content, thereby saving time and increasing efficiency. The continued integration of AI in NLP holds immense potential for the future, promising even more sophisticated and intuitive language processing capabilities.

Machine learning and NLP, have a synergy between them that has revolutionized the way we approach language processing and analysis. Machine learning algorithms, particularly those based on neural networks, have enabled NLP systems to learn from vast amounts of data, continuously improving their understanding of human language. This evolution has had a profound impact on various applications, from predictive text and auto-correction in smartphones to more complex tasks like topic modeling and language generation.

One of the most notable impacts of machine learning in NLP is in the area of content recommendation. By analyzing user preferences, search history, and interaction patterns, NLP systems powered by machine learning can provide personalized content suggestions, enhancing user experience on platforms like news aggregators, streaming services, and e-commerce websites. Another significant application is in the field of natural language understanding, where machine learning models are trained to comprehend the intent behind user queries, enabling more accurate and relevant responses from chatbots and virtual assistants.

Furthermore, machine learning's role in NLP extends to the analysis of unstructured data, such as customer feedback and social media posts. By applying NLP techniques, businesses can extract valuable insights from this data, understanding customer sentiments, market trends, and even identifying potential areas of improvement in products or services. The combination of machine learning and NLP also facilitates more efficient document classification and organization, aiding in information retrieval and knowledge management across various industries.

The integration of NLP in voice assistance technologies has ushered in a new era of human-computer interaction. Voice assistants, powered by NLP, are now capable of understanding and responding to spoken commands and queries in a natural and intuitive manner. This advancement has made voice assistants a ubiquitous presence in many aspects of daily life, from setting alarms and reminders to providing weather updates and news briefings. The evolution of voice assistance has also seen the incorporation of personalized responses, where the assistant adapts its responses based on the user's preferences and past interactions, making the experience more engaging and user-friendly.

Smart home technology sees the ability to have voice assistants become central to the operation of various devices and systems. They allow users to control lighting, temperature, security, and entertainment systems through voice commands, simplifying the management of the home environment. This has not only enhanced convenience but also accessibility, enabling individuals with mobility or visual impairments to interact more easily with technology.

The future of voice assistance in NLP is geared towards more advanced capabilities like context-awareness and anticipatory computing. Voice assistants are being developed to understand the context of a conversation and provide responses that are relevant to the current situation or environment. Anticipatory computing, on the other hand, involves voice assistants predicting user needs and providing information or taking actions proactively, based on learned patterns and behaviors. These advancements will further streamline user interaction with technology, making it more seamless and intuitive.

The convergence of NLP and computer vision is one of the most exciting developments in AI, offering a holistic approach to understanding and interpreting the world around us. By combining the capabilities of NLP to process language with computer vision's ability to analyze visual data, AI systems can now provide richer and more comprehensive insights. This integration plays a crucial role in areas such as accessibility, where visually impaired individuals can benefit from descriptions of their surroundings provided in natural language.

In the field of content analysis, the combination of NLP and computer vision is transforming how we interact with multimedia content. AI systems can analyze images and videos, extract relevant information, and then use NLP to describe this content in a human-like manner. This technology is not only enhancing user experiences on social media and digital platforms but is also invaluable in industries such as journalism and marketing, where quick and accurate analysis of visual content is essential.

Furthermore, the integration of NLP and computer vision is pivotal in the development of intelligent surveillance systems. These systems can monitor video feeds in real-time, identify and interpret actions, objects, and events, and then articulate these observations in natural language. This capability is immensely beneficial for security purposes, as it allows for quicker and more accurate responses to potential threats or unusual activities.

The incorporation of NLP into robotics has marked a significant leap in the field of robotics, leading to the creation of robots that can understand and respond to human language. This advancement has opened up new possibilities for interaction between humans and robots, making them more accessible and user-friendly. In industrial settings, robots equipped with NLP can receive and understand verbal instructions, allowing for more flexible and dynamic operation. This capability is particularly useful in environments where quick adaptation to new tasks or conditions is necessary.

In the healthcare sector, the integration of NLP in robotics is proving to be a game-changer. Robots can now assist in patient care, not only by performing routine tasks but also by engaging in therapeutic interactions. For instance, robots can provide reminders for medication, assist in physical therapy, and even offer companionship to patients, especially the elderly. This not only improves the quality of care but also reduces the workload on healthcare professionals.

Educational robots, empowered with NLP, are transforming the learning experience for students. These robots can engage students in interactive language learning, assist in problem-solving, and provide personalized educational support. The use of NLP in educational robots makes learning more engaging and effective, as it allows for a more natural and interactive form of communication between the robot and the student.

The integration of NLP with the Internet of Things (IoT) is a significant step towards creating smarter and more interactive environments. In smart home ecosystems, IoT devices equipped with NLP capabilities can understand and act upon voice commands, making the management of home appliances and systems more intuitive and convenient. This technology not only enhances the functionality of these devices but also makes them more accessible to a wider range of users, including those with physical disabilities.

Natural language processing-enabled IoT devices can contribute to more efficient and sustainable urban management. For example, IoT sensors can collect data on traffic, pollution levels, and energy usage, and then use NLP to communicate this information in an understandable and actionable manner. This can lead to better decision-making in areas such as traffic management, environmental monitoring, and resource allocation.

The integration of NLP and IoT also has significant implications for industries such as agriculture and manufacturing. In agriculture, IoT devices can provide farmers with voice-activated access to information about weather conditions, soil health, and crop status. In manufacturing, IoT sensors can monitor machinery and processes, with NLP enabling workers to interact with these systems through natural language, improving efficiency and safety in the workplace.

Virtual Reality enhanced with NLP capabilities is redefining digital engagement by creating more immersive and interactive experiences. In the gaming industry, this integration allows players to navigate and interact with the virtual world using voice commands. This not only makes gameplay more intuitive but also opens up new possibilities for game design, where players can influence the gameplay and outcomes through their spoken interactions.

In the field of education, VR combined with NLP offers innovative ways to learn and practice new skills. Language learning applications in VR, for example, can simulate real-world conversational scenarios, allowing learners to practice speaking and listening in a controlled, immersive environment. This approach to language learning is not only more engaging but also provides immediate feedback, enhancing the learning process.

The use of NLP in VR also extends to professional training and simulation. For instance, medical students can practice surgical procedures in a virtual environment, receiving voice-guided instructions and feedback. This type of training is invaluable, as it allows for the safe and repeated practice of complex tasks, preparing students for real-life situations in a risk-free setting.

Augmented Reality integrated with Natural Language Processing is transforming the way we interact with our environment, offering a fusion of digital and physical realms. This integration is especially impactful in sectors like tourism and navigation. Tourists, for instance, can use AR and NLP-enhanced applications to interact with historical sites in their native language, receiving real-time information and stories about landmarks. In navigation, AR with NLP can revolutionize the experience by providing voice-guided directions overlaid on the real world, making navigation more intuitive and engaging, especially in complex urban environments.

In the field of healthcare, AR combined with NLP is opening doors for innovative patient education and support. Medical professionals can use AR applications to explain complex medical conditions and procedures to patients in a more interactive and understandable manner. Patients, through voice commands, can query these AR systems for clarifications or additional information, making medical advice more accessible and personalized. This technology is particularly beneficial in areas like physiotherapy, where AR can guide patients through exercises while NLP processes their feedback or questions in real-time, ensuring correct posture and technique.

The integration of AR and NLP is also playing a crucial role in enhancing accessibility for individuals with disabilities. For people with hearing impairments, AR and NLP technology can convert spoken language into text or sign language animations in real-time, facilitating communication in a way that was not previously possible. Similarly, individuals with visual impairments can benefit from NLP-powered AR systems that describe their surroundings, helping them navigate spaces more independently and safely.

In the healthcare sector, the synergy between robotics and Natural Language Processing is pioneering a new paradigm in patient care and medical procedures. Robots equipped with NLP are enhancing patient engagement and care management. For instance, in mental health care, NLP-driven robots are being used for therapeutic conversations with patients, providing a level of interaction and support that supplements human care. These robots can recognize verbal and non-verbal cues, allowing them to respond in a way that is empathetic and tailored to the individual patient's emotional state.

In the area of eldercare, robotics integrated with NLP technology is proving to be invaluable. These robots can assist elderly individuals with daily tasks, remind them to take medications, and provide company, thereby reducing the feeling of loneliness. They can engage in natural language conversations, understand the needs of the elderly, and even detect signs of distress or health issues, alerting caregivers when necessary. This technology not only enhances the quality of life for the elderly but also provides peace of mind for their families and caregivers.

Furthermore, robotics and NLP are revolutionizing medical training and education. Medical robots can simulate patient interactions, allowing medical students to practice their diagnostic and communication skills in a realistic yet controlled environment. These simulations, powered by NLP, can mimic a wide range of patient scenarios and responses, providing future healthcare professionals with a diverse and comprehensive training experience. This integration of technology in medical education is preparing a new generation of healthcare providers with enhanced skills in patient communication and care.

Quantum computing, with its promise to redefine the capabilities of NLP, emerges as a natural progression from the advancements seen in robotics and NLP. It's anticipated to take the baton from these existing technologies, enabling more complex NLP tasks such as contextual analysis and predictive modeling. The potential of quantum computing to enhance language models extends far beyond the current boundaries, offering depth and accuracy that could transform AI conversational agents and language understanding systems. This leap from simulated patient interactions in medical training to advanced language processing in quantum computing marks a significant stride in the journey of technological advancement in healthcare and beyond.

Multilingual communication and quantum computing could provide a significant breakthrough. It has the potential to enable real-time, accurate translation between multiple languages simultaneously, overcoming the limitations of current translation technologies. This would not only enhance global communication but also contribute significantly to breaking down language barriers in international business, diplomacy, and cross-cultural exchange.

However, the advent of quantum computing in the field of NLP also brings forth complex challenges, particularly in the areas of data security and ethical use. The immense processing power of quantum computers could render current encryption methods obsolete, raising concerns about the privacy and security of sensitive language data. Therefore, the development of quantum computing in NLP must be accompanied by robust cybersecurity measures and ethical guidelines to ensure that these advanced technologies are used responsibly and for the benefit of society. The ethical considerations also extend to the potential for misuse in areas such as surveillance and propaganda, emphasizing the need for a balanced approach that weighs technological advancements against societal impacts and ethical implications.

The intricacies of NLP and AI, shows us a profound argument unfolding - the potential of this technological amalgamation to revolutionize our world is not just imminent, it is inevitable. The journey from robotic simulations in medical training to the advanced language processing capabilities promised by quantum computing paints a picture of a future where the limitations of human language are no longer barriers, but bridges to uncharted territories of innovation and understanding. The narrative reaches its climax in the prospect of quantum-enhanced NLP, a leap that could transform multilingual communication, shattering the age-old barriers of language and culture.

Yet, this evolution is not without its challenges. As we stand on the precipice of this new era, we grapple with ethical dilemmas and security concerns. The responsibility lies in our hands to steer this technological revolution towards a future that benefits humanity, ensuring that the power of quantum computing and NLP is harnessed with conscience and responsibility. This chapter leaves us not just with a sense of awe at the possibilities but also with a feeling of wholeness and readiness. Ready to embrace a future where AI and NLP work in tandem to create a world more connected, more understood, and profoundly more human.

Chapter 18

Speaking the Language of Emotion in a Digital World

Imagine a world where your digital assistant not only understands your words but also your emotions, where your chatbot advisor provides financial guidance with a personal touch. How will this transformation of Natural Language Processing redefine our interactions, both with technology and each other? This chapter will continue to unveil how natural language processing is defining a future where conversations with machines are as natural and intuitive as talking to a friend.

Consider the tale of "Eva," a sophisticated chatbot deployed by a leading bank. Initially programmed to handle simple transactions, Eva evolved through NLP advancements to offer personalized financial advice, understanding customers' needs and emotions. This story, reaching its climax later in the chapter, illustrates the profound impact of NLP in transforming not just customer service but the very fabric of human-machine interaction.

The evolution of chatbot technology marks a significant milestone in the journey of Natural Language Processing. Initially constrained to scripted responses, today's chatbots exhibit a level of interaction indistinguishable from human conversations. A pivotal example of this evolution is the transformation of customer service chatbots. Initially limited to answering FAQs, they now engage customers in intricate dialogues, providing personalized recommendations and solving complex queries with human-like empathy and understanding. This leap in sophistication is attributed to advances in NLU (Natural Language Understanding) and NLG (Natural Language Generation), allowing chatbots to process user inputs more accurately and generate contextually relevant responses.

One notable example is the use of chatbots in the banking sector. Banks have employed advanced chatbots that not only assist customers with transactions and inquiries but also offer financial advice based on individual spending habits and saving goals. These chatbots analyze user data to provide customized financial planning, transforming the banking experience.

Looking to the future, chatbot technology is poised to become even more sophisticated. The integration of emotional intelligence, allowing chatbots to recognize and respond to user emotions, is an emerging trend. This advancement will enable chatbots to provide support that is not only informative but also empathetic, significantly enhancing user experience. Another future trend is the development of multilingual chatbots, which can communicate in several languages, breaking language barriers and making digital platforms more accessible to a diverse global audience.

However, these advancements come with challenges. Ensuring that chatbots are unbiased and respect user privacy is paramount. Developers must focus on creating inclusive and ethical AI systems by diversifying training datasets and implementing rigorous privacy protocols. The potential for chatbots is immense, and they are set to revolutionize not just business operations but also how organizations interact and build relationships with their customers.

Voice-activated assistants, like Amazon Alexa and Google Assistant, have initiated a paradigm shift in human-computer interaction. Leveraging ASR (Automatic Speech Recognition) and NLU, these assistants have made significant strides in understanding and responding to diverse linguistic patterns, accents, and dialects. An exemplary instance of this evolution is seen in smart home devices. Voice-activated assistants enable users to control various aspects of their homes, from playing music to adjusting thermostats, using simple voice commands. This convenience has redefined the concept of a smart, interconnected home.

Beyond smart homes, these assistants are making inroads into areas like elderly care. Voice-activated systems provide seniors with a way to interact with technology effortlessly, offering them reminders for medication, emergency communication options, and even companionship through interactive conversations.

The future of voice-activated assistants lies in their integration with other technological domains. For example, coupling these assistants with IoT (Internet of Things) could lead to more comprehensive home automation systems that not only respond to voice commands but also anticipate user needs based on their habits and preferences. Another area of growth is in customization and personalization, where these systems will offer more tailored experiences by understanding individual user preferences and interaction patterns.

However, this advancement in voice-activated technology brings challenges in terms of privacy and security. Ensuring the confidentiality of voice interactions and safeguarding against unauthorized access are crucial concerns that developers need to address. As these assistants become more ingrained in our daily lives, striking a balance between convenience and privacy will be essential.

The integration of emotional intelligence in NLP systems represents a significant leap in humanizing machine interaction. Emotionally intelligent machines can interpret and respond to human emotions, offering a level of empathy that enhances user experience. In customer service, for instance, emotionally intelligent chatbots can detect customer frustration or satisfaction, tailoring their responses to improve the interaction. This capability is particularly valuable in managing complex customer interactions, leading to higher satisfaction and loyalty.

Healthcare sees emotionally intelligent NLP systems being used for mental health applications. These systems can detect subtle cues in a patient's speech or text, providing timely support or alerting healthcare professionals in cases of severe emotional distress.

The development of empathetic NLP systems, while promising, presents an expansive topic filled with technical and ethical complexities. The task of accurately interpreting human emotions from text or speech involves developing sophisticated models trained on a broad spectrum of data. Moreover, there is an ethical dimension to consider. The fine line between providing empathetic support and encroaching on personal emotions is a crucial navigational point for developers. The goal is to enhance the user experience with these systems, ensuring they offer support without infringing on privacy or personal autonomy.

Looking forward, the future of emotionally intelligent NLP systems is anchored in their ability to evolve with each interaction. As these systems become more sophisticated, they promise to deliver increasingly personalized and empathetic exchanges. This progression is gradually narrowing the gap between human and machine communication, making interactions more seamless and intuitive.

Taking a step further, the development of context-aware NLP systems marks a significant leap towards replicating human-like interactions in the digital domain. These systems, by grasping the context in which interactions occur, can provide responses that are not just accurate but also uniquely tailored to the individual user. For instance, a context-aware virtual assistant, leveraging insights from a user's past preferences and current circumstances, can offer travel recommendations that are both relevant and personalized. This level of understanding elevates the user experience, offering a glimpse into a future where digital interactions are as nuanced and adaptive as human conversations.

In e-commerce, context-aware chatbots enhance the shopping experience by remembering past interactions and preferences, recommending products accordingly. This level of personalization not only improves user experience but also drives sales by offering relevant products.

Developing context-aware systems, however, poses unique technical challenges. Understanding context requires sophisticated algorithms capable of processing and remembering past interactions, user preferences, and external factors like location and time. This necessitates advanced machine learning models and extensive data, which must be handled responsibly to protect user privacy.

Looking ahead, the future of context-aware NLP systems is promising. As these systems become more sophisticated, they will offer increasingly personalized and relevant experiences, further enhancing the usability and appeal of digital platforms. However, developers must remain vigilant about user privacy and data security, ensuring that personalization does not come at the cost of user trust.

Multilingual NLP is revolutionizing communication by breaking language barriers. This technology enables seamless conversation between individuals speaking different languages, fostering understanding and collaboration. An impressive example of this is in global customer service, where multilingual chatbots can assist customers in their native language, enhancing the customer experience and expanding market reach.

In education, multilingual NLP facilitates language learning by providing real-time translation and language practice, making language education more accessible and effective. For businesses, it allows for expansion into new markets by offering multilingual support, essential in today's globalized economy.

Developing accurate and culturally sensitive multilingual NLP systems presents significant challenges. Capturing the nuances and idiomatic expressions of different languages requires not just advanced algorithms but also an understanding of cultural contexts. This necessitates collaboration between technologists and cultural experts to create systems that are not only linguistically accurate but also culturally appropriate.

The future of multilingual NLP shines with promise, offering a panorama of applications across numerous sectors. As these technologies continue to evolve, we anticipate an era where their accuracy and ubiquity enhance global communication, breaking down language barriers and fostering a more inclusive exchange of ideas and information.

Yet, as we embrace these technological strides, the imperative of social responsibility in NLP development becomes increasingly evident. A key aspect of this responsibility is addressing and mitigating bias within NLP systems. Biases, if unaddressed, can lead to outcomes that are discriminatory and counterproductive to the goal of inclusivity. To ensure these technologies serve society equitably, developers must adopt proactive strategies. This includes diversifying the datasets used for training these systems and implementing regular audits of algorithms to uncover and rectify biases. Such measures are crucial not only for building fair and just NLP systems but also for maintaining public trust in these technologies. By aligning technological advancements with ethical practices, we can ensure that multilingual NLP systems not only connect the world through language but also uphold the values of equity and fairness in the digital age.

Developers and companies can take actionable steps to promote socially responsible NLP. This includes engaging with diverse groups during the development process to understand different perspectives, implementing transparency in algorithmic decision-making, and ensuring that NLP systems are accessible to people from all backgrounds.

Ethical considerations in NLP also extend to user privacy and data security. Companies must prioritize protecting user data and be transparent about how data is used. This involves not only technical measures but also adherence to ethical guidelines and legal frameworks.

The commitment to socially responsible NLP transcends mere technological innovation. It's about sculpting a future where digital tools embody fairness and inclusivity. As NLP technologies mature, anchoring them in ethical practices ensures they contribute positively to society at large, supporting a future where digital advancements are synonymous with social betterment.

This ethos is mirrored in the rise of conversational interfaces, now a staple in daily interactions. These interfaces, embedded in devices such as smartphones and smart home systems, have revolutionized how we engage with technology. By enabling interactions through natural language, these systems have made technology more approachable and user-centric. The simplicity and efficiency they offer reflect the broader objective of technology serving as an enabler, improving productivity and enhancing the user experience. This progression towards intuitive, conversational technology not only demonstrates NLP's practical applications but also underscores its role in making technology a seamless and inclusive part of everyday life.

In the workplace, conversational interfaces streamline workflows by allowing employees to interact with systems and access information through simple voice or text commands. This improves efficiency and reduces the time spent on routine tasks.

For individuals with disabilities, conversational interfaces can be life-changing. They offer an accessible way to interact with technology, enabling independence and improving quality of life. For example, voice-activated systems allow visually impaired users to access information and control devices without the need for visual cues.

The future of conversational interfaces is promising, with advancements in NLP making these systems more intuitive and responsive. As these interfaces become more sophisticated, they will further integrate into our daily lives, enhancing our interaction with technology and making digital experiences more natural and efficient.

In the novel era of advanced conversational systems, the intertwining of security and privacy with technological innovation is more critical than ever. These systems, which often handle sensitive personal data, are not immune to security challenges and breaches, underscoring the importance of robust protective measures. Recent incidents in conversational AI, including data leaks and unauthorized access, have highlighted vulnerabilities that could compromise user trust.

To tackle these challenges, developers and companies are employing state-of-the-art encryption techniques and secure communication channels. This approach is vital in safeguarding data in transit and at rest, thus maintaining the integrity and confidentiality of user information. Moreover, the design of these systems increasingly prioritizes ethical considerations, focusing on transparency around data usage and ensuring users retain control over their personal information.

The concept of privacy by design is becoming a cornerstone in the development of conversational systems. Techniques such as data anonymization and pseudonymization are being employed to minimize risks associated with data handling. Regular security audits and compliance with legal frameworks like GDPR and HIPAA reinforce the commitment to data protection.

Balancing innovation in NLP with privacy concerns is an ongoing challenge. As conversational systems evolve, so too must the strategies for protecting user data. This dynamic process ensures these systems remain powerful tools for modern living, while also acting as bastions of user trust and safety.

The future of NLP research and development is poised at an exciting juncture, marked by emerging technologies and collaborative models that promise to push the boundaries of what's currently possible. One of the most notable emerging technologies is GPT-3, an advanced language processing AI that demonstrates an unprecedented ability to generate human-like text. GPT-3's capabilities in creating coherent and contextually relevant text have opened new avenues for NLP applications.

Quantum computing also stands as a groundbreaking development in the NLP field. Its potential to process and analyze vast amounts of language data at incredible speeds could revolutionize NLP tasks, from translation to sentiment analysis. The combination of quantum computing and NLP could lead to breakthroughs in language understanding and generation.

Collaboration is pivotal in the dynamic field of Natural Language Processing. Successful partnerships between academia, industry, and government are propelling this technology forward. These collaborations bring together diverse resources and expertise, creating fertile grounds for innovative ideas to flourish.

The collective endeavor in this technology's research and development transcends technological progress, aiming to bridge the communication divide between humans and machines. As we look ahead, a commitment to responsible and collective advancement in this field will undoubtedly shape the future of human-machine interaction.

The transformative effect of this technology in redefining communication and its profound societal impact is immense. As we move towards this conversational future, stakeholders from various sectors are encouraged to actively engage with and integrate this technology into their operational frameworks. This integration is crucial for staying competitive in a digitally-driven environment.

For businesses, implementing advanced tools like chatbots can significantly elevate customer experiences. In education, this technology supports personalized learning journeys. In healthcare, it contributes to more responsive and nuanced care.

To fully leverage the potential of this technology, ongoing learning and development are necessary. Professionals must enhance their skills to effectively implement these solutions, while organizations should cultivate environments conducive to innovation. This chapter is an invitation to join a transformative movement, where curiosity and advancement in this technology contribute to reshaping our world.

As we progress into this future, maintaining a commitment to ethical practices is essential. Ensuring that our technological advancements in this field align with values of fairness and respect is critical. This commitment guarantees that our progress enriches human connection and understanding.

Throughout this chapter, we've explored the advancements of this technology, from empathetic chatbots to context-aware virtual assistants, marking a transformative period in human-computer interaction. The evolution of chatbot technology, illustrated by the development of "Eva," showcases the transition from rigid, script-based responses to dynamic, emotionally intelligent interactions, signifying a significant advancement in digital communication.

Voice-activated assistants, once a novelty, have now become integral in our daily routines, redefining convenience and accessibility. They represent a shift towards a future where technology understands us more profoundly. The development of empathetic systems, despite its technical and ethical challenges, promises a future where digital interactions are not only efficient but also emotionally resonant.

Context-aware conversations and multilingual capabilities in these systems are eliminating barriers, making digital experiences more personalized and inclusive. The pursuit of socially responsible technology, addressing biases and promoting fairness, reflects our dedication to ethical technological progress.

This chapter concludes with this call to action; for ongoing engagement with advancements in this technology. It invites professionals, businesses, and individuals to be part of a conversational future that is fair, inclusive, and transformative. As we adopt these advancements, we must adhere to ethical standards, ensuring that our progress not only enhances communication but also deepens human connections. This marks the beginning of a conversational renaissance, where the blend of human intellect and artificial intelligence unveils new possibilities in our interaction with the world.

About the Author's

Aaron Gear

Not just a name, but a brand synonymous with versatility, innovation, and leadership in multiple industries. With a rich background that spans the entertainment industry, business, law enforcement, marketing, and government contracting, Aaron's expertise is both broad and extense. His journey in the entertainment sector, particularly in set and prop design construction, has given him unique insights that he often shares through his insightful blogs. These writings, which also cover topics like business, law enforcement, marketing, and inuence, have become a source of inspiration for many.

Jeremy Schreifels

   A versatile creative force, educator, and entrepreneurial guide. With a foundation in drumming and a air for songwriting, he seamlessly transitioned into international music production, crafting harmonious blends that bridge cultures. Jeremy's journey extended into authorship, where his words inspire and enlighten. A seasoned coach, he empowers entrepreneurs to channel creativity into business success. Jeremy's milestones, from performing with renowned musicians to coaching business owners, reect his dedication to integrity, passion, and the boundless possibilities of the creative spirit.

www.ingramcontent.com/pod-product-compliance
Lightning Source LLC
LaVergne TN
LVHW051433050326
832903LV00030BD/3065